Qualify in Management

Qualify in Management

A workbook to get you through your management course

Mike Worsam

Croner Publications Ltd
Croner House
London Road
Kingston upon Thames
Surrey KT2 6SR
Tel: 01-547 3333

Copyright © 1989 Mike Worsam
This edition first published 1989

Published by
Croner Publications Ltd,
Croner House,
London Road,
Kingston upon Thames,
Surrey KT2 6SR
Telephone 01-547 3333

All rights reserved.
No part of this publication may be reproduced,
stored in a retrieval system, or transmitted in any form or by
any means, electronic, mechanical, photocopying, recording,
or otherwise,
without prior permission of
Croner Publications Ltd.

While every care has been taken
in the writing and editing of this book,
readers should be aware that only Acts of Parliament
and Statutory Instruments have the force of law,
and that only the courts can authoritatively
interpret the law.

British Library Cataloguing in Publication Data

Worsam, Mike
Qualify in management.
1. Management
I. Title
658

ISBN 1-85452-022-9

Printed by Whitstable Litho Ltd,
Whitstable, Kent.

This is not a textbook — its sole purpose is to help students secure a management qualification.

This book concentrates upon management courses offered by colleges and polytechnics. It will be of benefit to all students taking "internally assessed" courses.

Using the BTEC Certificate in Management Studies and the NEBSM Certificate in Supervisory Management as models, it shows how a student may secure a pass with minimum effort.

It explains how the courses are evaluated; shows students how to turn their natural apprehension into a positive benefit; and encourages each student to formulate his or her own preferred method for securing a pass.

THE AUTHOR

Mike Worsam is a Principal Lecturer at Croydon College. He has been in education for twelve years, and has taught both management and marketing to CMS and NEBSM students. He has set and marked many examinations for courses from "A" to Post Graduate level and he has been responsible for the evaluation of courses where continuous assessment criteria apply.

For 10 years he has been closely involved with the Commercial Education Scheme of the London Chamber of Commerce and Industry (LCCI). First as a Moderator for the LCCI/RSA/BTEC Joint Scheme; and for five years was responsible for the Third Level Diploma in Marketing. In this role he supervised the work of four Senior Examiners, their Assistant Examiners, and their Moderators.

(The LCCI set a truly international standard, and their qualifications are highly regarded from Hong Kong to Liverpool.)

As a tutor, Mike has coached students taking management and marketing courses. He is particularly well qualified in the pragmatic business of **getting students through**.

Contents

Introduction: Welcome to this Workbook   9

Acknowledgements   11

SECTION I — **Preparing yourself**
Chapter 1   Getting your pass   15
Chapter 2   Self-analysis   25
Chapter 3   Memory   33
Chapter 4   Learning   49
Chapter 5   Study skills   65

SECTION II — **The task you face**
Chapter 6   Management and management courses   75
Chapter 7   Continuous assessment explained   91
Chapter 8   Continuous assessment — the personalities   101
Chapter 9   Continuous assessment — its importance
              to students   113

SECTION III — **Course work**
Chapter 10   Success in assessments   125
Chapter 11   Personal development journal   137
Chapter 12   The project   147
Chapter 13   The residential weekend   175

SECTION IV — **The examination**
Chapter 14   Preparing to pass a written examination   191

Chapter 15	The day of the exam	199
Chapter 16	Your examination paper	207
Chapter 17	Question spotting	213
Chapter 18	Question answering	219
Chapter 19	Presenting your work	229
Chapter 20	The oral interview	239

SECTION V — **The key points**

| Chapter 21 | Summary | 249 |

Appendix A	Recommended reading	253
Appendix B	Moderator's Report Form	255
Appendix C	Examiners' reports	261
Appendix D	Examination terminology	267

Index 269

SPECIAL OFFER

Readers are invited to send for a representative selection of assignments *with tutor's notes* — see page 275 for details

Introduction

Welcome to this Workbook

This is one book in a series that takes a *practical* approach to student success. Qualifications are there to be gained — let's get it done! But let's do it the easy way! There is no need for the extremes of nervousness that so many students suffer. They can, and should, be avoided. This book shows how to achieve a management qualification that is awarded following a course of continuous assessment.

It takes the student through the entire process of the course, with practical examples carefully explained. It is for management students but it is **not** a management text; it is targeted at one thing only — showing management students how to achieve management qualifications.

There are four main sections:

1. **PREPARING YOURSELF:** the underlying principles — self-analysis, learning, memory, note taking, review, revision.

2. **THE TASK YOU FACE:** the assessment system, moderators and examiners are human (!), the importance of assessment to students.

3. **COURSEWORK:** how to succeed in coursework, how to

manage a personal development journal, how to write a project, what to expect on a residential weekend.

4. **THE EXAMINATION:** how a question paper is set and marked, why examiners prefer to pass candidates rather than fail them. Ensuring a pass in both written and oral exams.

Real examples, from real courses, are used. Reports from moderators and examiners are quoted. The easy way to qualify is spelled out very clearly.

Acknowledgements

A considerable debt is owed to Angela Hatton, David Jackson, Syd Cheeswright, David Pennyfather and Lynda Whaite who are management tutors at Croydon College. They have provided detailed facts and, more importantly, have gently pointed out my errors. Doubtless mistakes will creep into the printed book, for these I accept full responsibility...

I obviously wasn't listening, folks!

The author wishes to thank LCCI, BTEC, NEBSM, Tony Buzan and BBC Publications for permission to use copyright material.

Section One

Preparing Yourself

Chapter 1
Getting Your Pass

So you want to pass your course? Great! No problem.

No, really, no problem. What we have to do is find out what can get in the way of your passing — and also how you are mentally approaching your task. Then we can set about dealing with the situation.

Let's see if we can agree about some basic principles; clear the way as it were.

First — You are not the only person who is worried about coping with a course.
Second — Most people assume that projects and examinations are difficult.
Third — Most people won't face facts. (And won't say exactly what they mean.)
Fourth — The first three principles are *normal*.
Fifth — Doing well in coursework, projects and exams takes skills that can be learned.
Sixth — *You* have to pass. No-one can do it for you.
Seventh — You have had no time at school, college, poly or university that concentrated on teaching you to pass examinations.
Eighth — You also have had no time devoted to learning how to learn.
Ninth — *You* have to establish the best way of passing, for *you*.
Tenth — Together we *will* get your pass.

Remember — this book is targeted exclusively on getting you through your course — successfully.

This is *not* a book which you sit and read. That would be no good at all. That would only be advice, or "book learning". If the eighth principle applies you've had no instruction on learning to learn; so what good to *you* is a textbook on technique?

Success in a course depends upon a lot of factors that get muddled together. One secret is simply to unscramble the muddle and thoroughly understand each element that makes up the course.

Examination passing, for example, is a skill; a skill that can be learned just as you can learn to play tennis or badminton, to ride a horse, to swim, to play bridge, to dance. Some people do it better than others — but all can do it well enough.

It is *vital* to begin, here and now, with the thought that your course is a game. A game that has rules which you need to understand, but that is fun to play. A course that is fun is easy to pass — and any course can be fun if you want it to be.

The course may not be the "game" that you would choose, but it is the one that you have to play because it is the route to the qualification you need. No use complaining, no way to dodge. So let us get on with some basic understanding. We need to go over the principles from page 15 in more detail.

First principle — You are not the only person who is worried about coping with a course.

Why shouldn't a person feel worried about academic assessment? Our society has created such a myth around examinations, and puts such a value on certificates and diplomas, that there is bound to be pressure.

Pressure comes, in particular, from loved ones who, meaning well, insist on "revision" without any idea of what true revision is!

It comes from friends and colleagues, those also taking the same course, those who have taken it and passed. A different pressure comes from those who have failed!

Pressure comes from the subjects — they are all new to you, and their very complexity can be frightening at first. Pressure comes from yourself. You want to pass, you want to pass with no, or minimum effort — you are frightened you won't. A management student, in particular, has a very wide range of topics to cover. You will be better at some than others — this is normal, and *allowed for in the system*.

Anybody who isn't concerned or doesn't have some degree of fear, is in one of three situations: he or she hasn't yet appreciated how time must be managed; truly doesn't care if he or she passes or not; or is so insensitive that this book will be of no help.

NOTE: "Fear" may appear a dramatic word — but it describes the "extreme nervousness" of many students far better than any other. There is a *plus* side to fear (to nerves if you prefer) — from the fear comes strength. The body's natural reaction when we are frightened is to heighten our ability to cope with the danger. So the message is treasure your fear; learn how to benefit, *don't* be taken by surprise, and don't panic at exam time!

ACTION

Make a list, here and now, of the pressures that you may be under. (If in doubt about a pressure, leave it in.)

Technique: if you have come across mind maps, then use one. If not, make a list of the main areas and then itemise the individual pressures coming from each. (We shall come to mind map techniques later; for the moment don't worry if you don't yet know about them.)

Take about 20 minutes.

You should now have a first list of the pressures. (First list because you should add to it as other ideas strike you.) What should you do with it?

You will be able to group the pressures in some way — those coming from friends who have passed, for example. What is the best way, for *you*, to handle these? It could be that you should tackle them head on by asking for advice and assistance. Appeal to their pride, use a bit of flattery. Admit, to yourself, that they have passed, and that you intend to. Never be frightened of asking for help, you do *not* have to tackle your problems alone.

In some cases it will be necessary for you to build a protective skin around your self-confidence, and let the pressures bounce off. (It is possible to develop the skill of avoidance, so that the pressures go past — but it is hard to master the art.)

There are two reasons why your "pressure analysis" is important:

1. it lets you see exactly the size of your problem;

2. it allows you to come up with techniques for dealing with it.

Pressure won't go away, but it must be turned so that it is helpful rather than crippling. Parents are just great at putting on useless pressure. The typical student response is to shout, to sulk, to avoid the work to "spite them".

To spite them! Be careful of this one — the only person to suffer in the long run is yourself. So you have to work out a way of avoiding the problem. There are lots of possibilities, such as the following:

➤ Treat course work as real work, and go out to do it. Work in school or college, or in the public library.

➤ Work in a friend's house, share the workload, share the hassle!

► Involve parents. (They are desperate for you. Much of their problem is that they have to cope with you doing it by yourself, and they still remember you as a helpless baby.)

► Schedule your workload through the year, and at set times through each week.

► Let people see that you are working to a schedule, that you have a plan of action.

It is good to ask yourself *"What is the worst thing that could happen if I were to fail?"* Get that out into the open **now**, then you are more able to see exactly how important the course is, and therefore how much of your time and energy should be devoted to it.

Remember — **You are not the first, not the only, and certainly not the last person to be bothered about a course or about exams. But pass rates are extremely high *for those who prepare thoroughly*. In particular, note that if you have been selected for the course your tutor *expects* you to pass. Respect his or her judgement — tutors do not want their students to fail. They are paid to achieve passes!**

Second principle — Most people assume that projects and examinations are difficult.

Projects difficult? Examinations difficult? Nonsense! But they are *impossible* to those who have little knowledge of the subject, and no skills in exam technique. (We shall be looking at knowledge and skills a little later.)

It's pretty obvious (isn't it?) that fear adds to pressure, creates difficulty, leads to misunderstanding. And we are not helped by old wives' tales that are told about exams... especially by those who want to magnify their achievement in passing, ot diminish their guilt in failure!

Douglas Adams created the "Hitch Hiker's Guide to the Galaxy" and if he hadn't got there first I'd want to inscribe **DON'T PANIC** *on the cover of this book. You should adopt it as a firm instruction to yourself. Panic is the cause of so many bad exam results — get yours under control. (More later.)*

Third principle — Most people won't face facts. (And won't say exactly what they mean.)

Facing facts is difficult. One fact very hard to define is the truth about *yourself*. Only you can do it, listen to what other people say — but then think it through; are they correct? If so, what should you do about it? And what can you do about it?

If you should change, but really cannot, or don't want to, then fine... but be prepared for the consequences.

Students on a management course are often told in the opening session that "We don't mind if you are tough managers, or soft. That's your choice. But we do care that you are aware of the effects of your choice, and that you can cope with them".

You must be positive, and choose your course of actions — then live with them. But once you have chosen, you can also predict the reactions of others and select ways and means of coping with them.

The only **right** way is the **right** way for **you**.

Fourth principle — The first three principles are *normal.*

Simple enough? People keep up a front, you do too. But they are *all* apprehensive. Never, for a moment, believe otherwise.

The big difference for you is that you are going to be better prepared for each stage of your course than most of the others. You will go in with a much higher expectation of success.

Fifth principle — Doing well in course work, projects and exams takes skills that can be learned.

We are going to get on with some detailed work soon, but it is important first to establish a working relationship. It is not important that you agree with every word in the book, nor that you follow every piece of advice. It is **very important** that you see exactly what your problems are, and that you make plans — and carry them through — to make your task as easy as possible.

Course success *depends upon skills.* You can learn them. (They are every bit as important as learning your subject!) This book shows you exactly how to gain the skills that you need.

Sixth principle — *You* have to pass. No-one can do it for you.

You must be responsible for your own actions. You cannot blame anybody else if you fail. All the resources are available to you if you want to use them. There is an old saying that *"students pass despite their teachers"*. Many do because there are some pretty lousy teachers around. (Some pretty lousy bankers, builders and hairdressers as well!)

If you are stuck with a bad teacher why keep going to his or her classes? Would you be better off in the library? Will you try to change class or college? Or will you mumble to your friends, take extended coffee breaks, and waste learning time? **(And blame the teacher for your failure!)**

Why do you think he or she is a bad teacher anyway? Will you speak directly with him or her about it? Or will you chicken out and grumble, but do nothing positive?

*It is well known (or at least believed very widely) that law is a hard subject for non-legal students to learn. Time after time complaints are received about the quality of the law tutors — yet when followed through it turns out that the complaining students often haven't been to classes regularly, haven't even bought the necessary textbook! They copped out at the **idea** of learning law. They didn't even give it a fair run.*

Not everyone can be liked by everyone else. But in a professional relationship actual liking is a bonus. The acid test is "does this person know his or her material, and can I learn from him or her?"

Seventh principle — You have had no time at school, college, poly or university that concentrated on teaching you to pass examinations.

From age 5 to 16 you were in school. That is 11 years. 40 weeks a year is 440 weeks. 7 periods in a teaching day is 3080 periods.

How many of these were devoted to English? To maths? To art? (A great many.)

How many to exam technique? (Under ten? Immediately before an exam? Right?)

Note: in a management course that is internally assessed the examination will be only one part of the whole. You have to pass in coursework, and probably write a project as well. By the time you get through to the point of the examination you will have a lots of confidence based upon your results in the course work and project. We shall cover this thoroughly in Section Two.

Eighth principle — You also have had no time devoted to learning how to learn.

How many school periods were devoted to showing you how to learn? (In most cases — none!)

Learning is a subject that deserves time just as much as do the "normal" subjects. Each of us has an individual learning style, and a lot of research has been done to discover how people learn. This is normally not passed on to the students by their school teachers. Instead they have to learn it for themselves, the hard way, as they gain experience.

This book short-cuts that painful learning for you.

Ninth principle — YOU have to establish the best way of passing, for YOU.

Hopefully it is very clear that only *you* can pass, and that only *you* can decide how to do it. Each of us has a "best way" of learning. You must, with the help of this book, decide what is best for you — early morning, late at night; with or without music in the background; alone or in company... there are many combinations to select from.

Tenth principle — Together we *will* get your pass.

Work should be *fun*. (Really, it should.) There are 168 hours in every week. You have to choose how to use them. If you have to study a "boring" subject, then the best way is to concentrate and get it behind you, quickly. (It is a great feeling to know that it is over and done with!)

The principles and techniques you will learn from this book are all tried and tested. They have taken thousands and thousands of students through their courses and they will work for you. As a bonus they will help you to take the drudgery out of study.

SUMMARY

- Securing a management qualification is not difficult, given the right preparation.

- Preparation starts with self-analysis.

- Identify a series of actions that need to be taken.

- Determination is needed — to achieve a clear view of your own situation, to follow through on the plans that you make, and to live with the results of your actions.

- You must structure your time so that you use it productively.

- You need to learn about learning and about passing exams.

- *You* have to pass — no-one can do it for you.

- Study can and should be fun.

DETERMINATION IS A KEY TO QUALIFICATION.

Chapter 2
Self-Analysis

Let's do things in a sensible order. Before we can get down to any self-analysis we have to look how to analyse.

Analysis means *"resolution into simpler elements by examining the detailed constitution of..."* at this time the detailed constitution of yourself, but later we shall be using analysis techniques to plan answers for assignments and for exam questions. Once learned, these techniques will become routine and you will find yourself using them in your job and in your home life.

How did your problem analysis go in the last chapter? Do you have a page full of detail? Or do you have a list of headings that is not really detailed, nor complete, and certainly not useful? Or are you somewhere in between? No matter, providing you have made an attempt you have taken the first step towards being in charge of your own learning. (If you didn't try an analysis, do it right now, please.)

There are several ways to analyse a problem. The one selected for this book is the *"mind mapping"* technique. (It is fully described in Tony Buzan's book "Use Your Head".)

Most people, when asked to examine a problem, take a sheet of paper and make a list that starts at the top left hand corner and goes straight down. It is the obvious thing to do. But it does not fit in with the way that our brains work. We need a focus, a central point, around which to assemble our thoughts. Mind mapping uses the whole page, and starts in the centre.

Thus you are encouraged to spread out, to stretch, across the whole page. You will be surprised how this technique enables you to see connections and to avoid the blockages that come with the listing method. (Simply because one is looking at the problem as a whole, instead of trying to sort it out mentally before putting it on paper.) From a mind map you will easily be able to extract a simple list.

This book was planned using mind maps throughout.

In a moment you should take a blank sheet of paper and try a mind map for yourself — but first have a look at a map that helped in the planning of this book (see opposite page). You will see that each concept has a separate branch to itself and that each sub-idea branches from it. In your map you will probably find the same idea coming up on different branches. (That shows an interrelationship that may not have been caught in a simple list.) Obviously the map on page 27 has been tidied up, and you will tidy yours.

BASIC RULES

➤ Be brief – it is very hard at first, but it comes with practice.

➤ Always print.

➤ Use different colours for each branch to make it easy to see one whole topic at a glance.

➤ Let the map take whatever shape it wants.

➤ Put in cartoons, diagrams, comments, as the mood takes you. (Funny or odd things are easier to remember.)

Now you take a blank sheet of paper (A3 if possible) and mind map the pressures you may be under. (Yes, that's right, repeat what you were asked to do in the last chapter. *Don't* look back.) Take about 20 minutes.

Self-Analysis

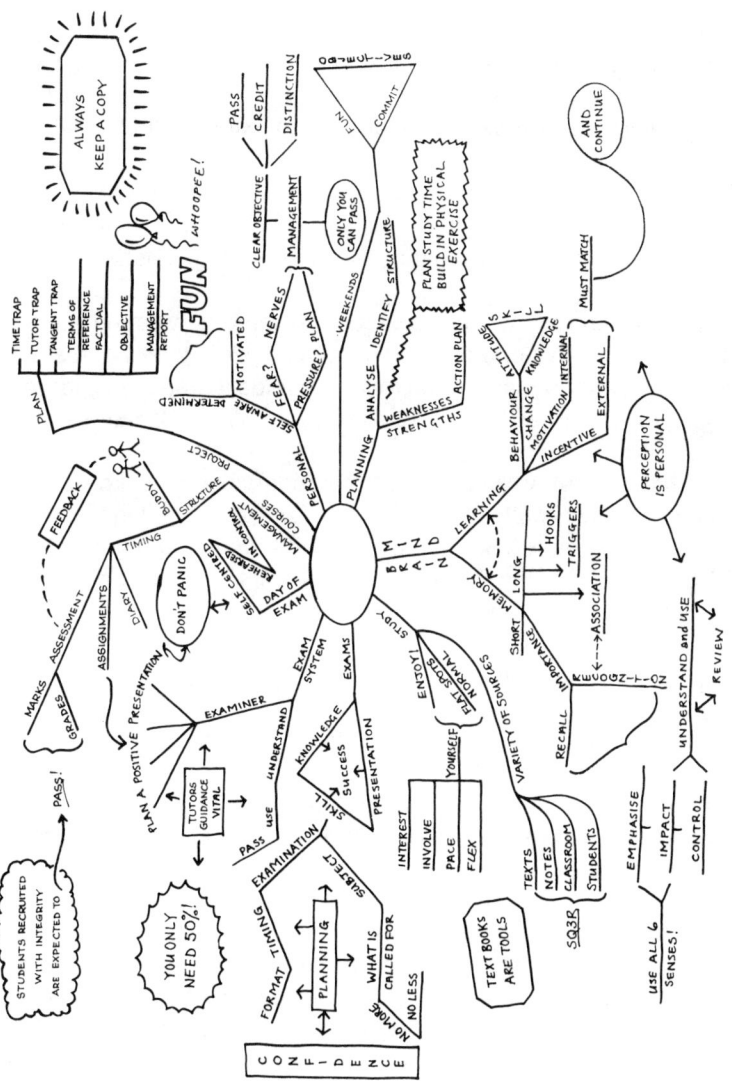

Mind map done? Good. Now have a very careful look at it and see how many actual pressures there are. (You will probably find that they can be grouped so that, for example, the worry of having to say you've failed is the same for friends and work mates, but different for bosses and parents.) At this stage you should be making a "normal" list. Compare it to your first list — it should be better. Is it?

The mapping technique helps one to produce an analysis of a situation and to rank the priorities in it. It is very efficient, but — like riding a bicycle — it is not an automatic skill. One has to persist.

Put your pressures list to one side for the moment, we need one other analytical tool. This one calls for some very clear thinking. It sounds much easier to do than a mind map, but to do it properly is, for many people, much harder. It is a STRENGTHS and WEAKNESSES analysis.

It is what it says. An analysis of the strengths and weaknesses of a given situation. Simply take a sheet of A4 and divide it in two across the centre. In the top part write STRENGTHS, in the bottom WEAKNESSES. Now be very honest with yourself and build mind maps of your own personal strengths and weaknesses.

What you should have is a list of at least 12 strengths, and as many weaknesses. Most often a strength has a balancing weakness right there on the same page: one can be very decisive (strength), but also intolerant (weakness). Strengths and weaknesses are often mirror images of each other.

It seems obvious, but many people miss the point that having analysed an area it is necessary to turn the data into useful information *and to take action.* You need to consolidate your strengths (improve them, toughen them up, learn to trust them, become self-confident about them). You need to work on your weaknesses (either by avoiding situations where a weakness will be damaging to you or your work or, better, by learning how to make an area less weak — how to get it up at least to average standard).

Self-Analysis

A lot of people want to lose weight, or to give up drinking. They do a lot of talking about it, but never actually really try. Never with a planned programme, never with outside help that understands and can set realistic standards of achievement. Yet Weightwatchers and Alcoholics Anonymous are two organisations that know how to help people solve their weight or drinking problems. Perhaps the key is in really wanting? You certainly have to really want to pass your course.

Now it is time to use your analyses. From your first mind map you came up with a list of your pressures. Use your strengths and weaknesses analysis to identify how to handle each particular pressure, Note actions to consolidate your strengths, and actions to minimise the effect of your weaknesses. Come up with one final list — the **action list**.

The action list is not a mind map. The mapping will have extracted data from your mind and shown you cross links which you would not otherwise have found. Now you need to put that data together in a form that enables you to use it.

The **action list** has three headings:

Pressure	Action to be taken	By when

It is a serious, working document. You should be able to see exactly what you need to do to handle the pressures you are going to be under. You should note if you do not have the capability to handle a pressure on your own. If this applies to you there are only three alternatives:

(a) give up the course,
(b) suffer the pressure, and risk the failure,
(c) get some outside help.

29

Help is available. Tutors, in the main, go into education because they get a great deal of satisfaction from helping students. (It is a great thrill when a student passes, especially when he or she has had problems with the subject.) So seek one out with whom you feel some rapport and talk the problem through. Or go to a college counsellor, who will certainly have met your problem before. The Students' Union is also very helpful.

Perhaps your employer will help, your uncle, a family friend? Often what you need is a person with a detached view who can help *you* to see *your* way through *your* problem.

Whatever you do, don't just accept the situation. Take action to rectify it.

The final point is to review and update your action list at least weekly. Making a definite time on a specific day is a good way not to forget. The important thing is to see just how well you are doing. You will find your list changing as you pass from week to week. In time you will be working on detailed points because you will have discovered precisely where you need to target your attention.

SUMMARY

➤ Be honest with yourself — evaluate your personal strengths and weaknesses.

➤ Consolidate your strengths.

➤ Work at improving and/or protecting your weaknesses.

➤ Practise the skills of mind mapping.

➤ Adopt an *active* view of life. Make your own way. Be responsible for your own learning.

➤ Review your progress, and amend your action list.

ABOVE ALL — BE HONEST WITH YOURSELF.

Chapter 3
Memory

If you are to pass your exam you must know something about your chosen subject, only just enough maybe, but enough. Agreed? OK — but knowing it, and being able to recall it when needed, are two different things. In fact, to know it you have to be able to learn it in the first place.

So the ability to learn something, *and* to store it away so that it can be found when you need it, is very important. Especially to a student on a course!

It is absolutely necessary for you to understand and accept certain basic principles. That is what this chapter and the next are about: basic principles that are easy to learn and easy to use... yet are very, very effective and will help you personally. (Appendix A provides some useful references for those who want a detailed understanding.)

Can you answer these simple questions?

1. How many days are there in September?
2. What are the colours of the rainbow?
3. Do stalactites go up? Or down?
4. What are the four points of the compass, in order?
5. Do clocks go forward or back at the end of summertime?

Answers:

1. 30. (Thirty days hath September...)
2. Red, orange, yellow, green, blue, indigo, violet. (ROYGBIV, or Richard Of York Gave Battle In Vain.)
3. Down. (Tites come down!)
4. North, East, South, West. (Never Eat Shredded Wheat.)
5. Back. (Spring forward, fall backward.)

Wait a minute, what's going on? Silly questions with silly rhymes and phrases! Well, the questions are surely not silly if you need to know the answers to them. True, the answers are supported by silly rhymes and phrases; but stop for a moment and enquire why.

*Seriously, Why? Take a few minutes to consider this **important question**. We will come back to it in a little while.*

In the meantime, consider that although we have a conscious mind, there are other levels of mental activity that we usually refer to as "unconscious". We all have a part of our mental activity, the "autonomic" part, that takes care of routine things such as breathing. (If the brain wasn't monitoring routine functions they would stop, or get out of synchronisation.)

It makes no sense to have conscious control over routine, so we are only told on the conscious level when things begin to go wrong.

Between the autonomic and conscious level is at least one other subconscious level (a deeper mind if you prefer) that we can and do access from time to time. Inter-related with this (very over simplified) description of our mental processes we must consider short and long term memory.

It seems that we possess both short and long term memories, and that it is partly up to us to decide that some data is important enough to be long term rather than short. "Partly up to us" because if an experience has sufficient impact, is very important to us, it will be stored long term without our even knowing that we have it in our head (until we next need it).

Memory

This perhaps explains why one can sit in front of routine television for an evening and not remember what one saw the next morning; why glancing through the cartoon pages of a magazine can cause a smile, without being able to remember the joke to repeat to someone else.

It also perhaps helps to explain why "cramming" can be effective. Cramming facts into short-term memory will work — for most people, most of the time. But the effect is transitory, and, without understanding, most *facts* are useless in an examination.

A very important part of gaining an effective memory is to understand how your own personal mental processes work, and being sure to structure your learning so that memory potential is maximised.

We shall get on to this later, for now let us go back to those "silly" questions. Why do people use silly rhymes and jingles? Perhaps you will have reasoned your answer out something like:

People have been using rhymes and silly phrases for generations, so they must work. They must help people to remember. We must find rhymes, etc easier to remember for some reason. And people don't abandon them when adult, so even though they may appear childish they perhaps have to be taken more seriously than that.

In fact they do have to be taken more seriously than that. There is much evidence to show that people remember poetry easier than prose, and that nonsense is very hard to remember. (Now, be careful — what may appear nonsense can make perfect sense to a specialist. Especially in these days of acronyms.)

The memory works best when it can *associate* data. Thus "Never Eat Shredded Wheat" is an association of ideas that allows access from a range of sources to extract the points of the compass (North, East, South, West) from the memory in the correct order.

Also note that something absurd or exaggerated, is remembered more easily than routine or everyday things. The more ridiculous the image you can create to help the association, and therefore the memory, the easier it is to recall the data you need.

More easily remembered are concepts and principles *that people regard as important.*

Importance is certainly a major factor in memory retention:

An experiment with students entering a course at a college in the United Kingdom was conducted in the early 1980s. Whilst waiting to be enrolled, some students were divided into two rooms. One group was given a test and told that the results were important to their success on the course. The other was given the same test, but told that it was simply to fill time whilst waiting.

Testing of recall showed that immediately after the test both groups remembered the same amount. But the recall of one group fell off radically within minutes of the test. An hour later their recall was down to under half of the other group's. A day later it was approaching zero! The other group (chosen at random) were still able to recall results from the test a month later, with only a slight fall off in accuracy.

You've guessed it — those who were told that the test was important were the ones that remembered, and didn't forget as time passed.

How did you work out your answers to the questions? Perhaps you had to go to a reference book for some, but for most they probably "popped" in to your mind instantly. Did you ask yourself a question? Did you institute a search? Perhaps you did, but without conscious effort because your mind executed the search as a routine response to the question mark at the end of each sentence. (The Spanish, incidentally, put a question mark at both ends of a written question — thus the reader is alerted immediately that a question is about to be asked and the mind can go into active state.)

Did you "hook" the answer out ot your memory by a rhyme or a jingle? If so, who set up the hook that was ready and waiting for the trigger question? Perhaps it was a good teacher? Yourself, perhaps?

Memory

Recall has been mentioned. This is what most people regard as "memory" — the ability to extract facts from the mind, without apparent aid. But there is another important facet of memory — *recognition*.

Recognition operates when the memory is triggered by some outside event: an example will make it clear:

*It is common in marketing research to ask people what advertisements they saw on television the previous evening. Once that list has been made, a set of flash cards is shown to each respondent. These carry the logo of a product or the focus of a commercial. Respondents almost always **recognise** more than they **recall**.*

Thus it is vital to get point-of-sale material and product packaging that triggers recognition from prospective customers.

You can set up recognition aids for yourself when learning, and you will find when writing answers in the exam room that the answer to one question will often trigger points for inclusion in another. This is a major factor to be borne in mind when planning your exam answers; we come back to it in Chapter 18.

You will have noticed that there are some things you cannot forget, however much you try. In fact trying to forget appears to make the memory stronger, not weaker! (The best way to forget is not to even think about the subject. To deliberately occupy the mind with something else. In time, and it may be a long time, the force of the memory will weaken. It will have moved out of the area labelled "often used".)

There are several interesting approaches to the problem of memory that you ought to know about.

The mind seems to exist *within* the brain, and does not have a specific part of the brain dedicated to it. Rather, it seems to draw upon the electrical and/or chemical functioning of the brain to co-ordinate and compare stored memories and current perceptions.

Thus it exists rather like a software program inside a computer. The body is the computer case, the brain the computer components, the mind the operating programs. We, of course, are the computer operators.

We must not take the computer analogy too far, but it does serve as a useful guide. It shows that we are in charge and that what we want to happen is what *will* happen provided we learn to use our brains effectively.

There is a better analogy to help explain how the "software" in our heads is created and amended. The Earth was probably once very much like a child's mind at birth. It had a certain shape and that shape controlled the movement of everything that was directly associated with it. Wind blew across it and was deflected by mountains; water fell upon it and ran downhill to the sea; animal life moved across it and dug, tunnelled, built into and upon it. Think of all these as similar to our five senses, for they have an impact upon our brains from our very earliest moments of life.

It is their impact that creates change in our mental ability, in our levels of knowledge and skills and in our view of the world. (Just as water will channel itself a deep ravine through even the hardest rock, so data input and use creates channels in our minds. Just as wind and water undermine cliffs, and huge trees are blown away by a storm, so data transforms our levels of understanding and our approach to the world.

Think of information as flowing around the brain in routes, in channels. The more often data goes down a route the deeper that channel becomes. The more permanent the routing the easier it is to find and to follow.

The harder an object hits the earth the more of a dent it will make. It is the same with memory. The impact, the importance, of a piece of data will determine the size, and depth, of the space it occupies in the brain.

Impact can be achieved by ensuring that the material is *understood* for this necessitates the mental processing of data, not simple acceptance. *Use* of data automatically indicates a level of importance that the brain will register.

Larger marks are more easily seen than small ones.

The greater the space allocated to a topic, the easier it is to find and retrieve.

Ages old activity leaves marks that can still be seen today: note how aerial photography shows up the outline of prehistoric villages even though the land has been farmed for centuries.

In just such a fashion, some argue, all experience is stored. But simple storing of data is not enough. An effective memory is one which not only stores data, but presents it back to you when you need it.

BASIC PRINCIPLES TO IMPROVE EFFECTIVE MEMORY

➤ **Use as many senses as possible when learning.** This deliberate focussing of body resources onto one task alerts the brain to the fact that you consider this important, and that the brain had better store it where you can retrieve it easily.

➤ **Get the greatest impact behind your learning.** Passive reading is a *very* ineffective way of transferring data from book to brain.

➤ **Be sure you understand and use what you learn.** The Double U Principle of understanding and use is vital to memory. (We return to this in the next chapter.)

➤ **Review your "learned material" regularly.** Keep reminding the brain that it is still important, that it must not be wiped or written over by new experiences.

➤ **Control your mental filing system.** When adding to your store of knowledge consciously inform the brain that this new data belongs with, and is associated with, whatever already exists. Don't let your brain file data away without guidance and control from you.

Learning and memory are each useless without the other. Good memory is dependent on your learning style — which must present the material so that it can be stored and accessed by you.

To extract the full benefit from your brain you must use it as it wants to be used. It exists to serve you, and it works far below your level of consciousness to feed data to you. You are perfectly aware that things "pop into your mind", without you consciously asking for them. Why? It can only be because something in your mental processes triggered a request for "relevant data". A search was run and data presented, You can't stop this process but you can learn to exploit it for your benefit.

One way to achieve this is to put the data into the brain with convenient handles, or hooks, so that it can easily be recognised. Hence the "silly rhymes" which we find much easier to remember than logical language.

Perhaps the brain continues to operate at childhood level, even though we have "grown up". Whatever the reason it certainly pays to treat the brain as a happy toddler who gets as much joy out of coloured wrapping paper and boxes as from the presents in the boxes!

Advertisers make great use of learning theory:

Once we have seen a powerful television commercial a few times there is a need only for the punchline or theme tune. We then recall the whole commercial for ourselves. The commercial had impact, and one or more "hooks". Our brains do the rest, automatically, when triggered by the jingle. (Recognition has taken place, and our brain has hooked out the associated data, automatically.)

Memory

Every new experience is matched and/or tested against existing knowledge — and only if it doesn't fit do we have a problem. The problem, of course, is to decide whether the new or the old experience is the valid one. Giving up something one has believed in for years is notoriously hard to do, as we all know.

It seems that for the mind there is no real distinction between the data coming in from the five senses (touch, taste, sight, sound, smell) and that coming from stored memory and experience. Perception is very much conditioned by the individual. Personal preferences, likes, dislikes and an individual's bias will colour the material and its presentation. In other words different individuals presented with the same apparent data will not necessarily perceive it in the same way. Certainly you will spend time well if you learn to work with your existing knowledge: never let pre-conditioning block the consideration of new data.

Brian Tracy, of Tracy College, who has worked extensively in this area, says that **perception is recognition and the formulation of a plan of action**. *Thus, for Brian Tracy, perception is* **active** *and a distinct asset to the individual who will harness its power.*

The mind is a great processor of data, it can be very creative in blending data to achieve new and startling results. It can hang on persistently to wrong data. It can be a great ally or a great handicap. It is up to you and how you manage it.

To maximise your potential for remembering you must give the brain data in the form that it likes it best. It likes data sorted, "hooked", and wrapped up in lovely colours. It likes bright things, brash things. It hates dull and drab experiences. It goes to sleep when bored, and repetition of the same task bores it immensely. (That is why text book *reading* is of so little use.)

You should be setting up hooks and triggers when making notes on your subject. Build triggers in from the start. Set up a series of triggers to help you associate and remember.

Have you noticed that some points are repeated in this chapter? Is it annoying you? Good! Because annoyance is impact and impact helps you to remember. (Not annoyed? Don't worry — your brain should have noted the repetition and responded to it. But it is for you *now* to check that your brain hasn't filtered out the repetition — that it has recognised the importance of the points.)

A situation also produces an effect. You know how much more active your brain is when close to an exam. The excitement or the stress can have a positive effect on brain activity. Once you can recognise this as a major strength, you will be able to rely heavily upon it. You will be able to set up situations where your brain will work as though to a deadline; all you have to do is create a deadline of your own and make it a genuine one. The brain doesn't know any better (you control it) so if you send signals saying "this is *important*" the brain will respond. But you have to truly believe, right down into your subconscious, that it is important. (That is one reason why mock examinations are so valuable when properly set up and taken seriously by the candidates.)

One final point; the more we use our powers of recall and recognition, the more reliable they become. Trust your ability to remember but don't expect too much at first. Do expect more and more as your skill develops. It will develop and it will get better *and it won't go away when you need it.*

What you have to do is find out what works best for *you,* and package your learning to fit *your* needs. Always attach hooks and triggers at the time of learning.

Take 20 minutes on this exercise:

You have to remember to buy ten things in the supermarket during your lunchbreak tomorrow. They are: salad cream, butter, tea bags, kitchen roll, loaf of bread, sardines, pickles, chewing gum, chocolate, matches.

Your task is to devise hooks and triggers that will work for you. Ones

Memory

that make it possible for you to go to work tomorrow, without a written list, or reminder, and go shopping for these ten items.

There is no right answer. It can be done in many ways. You must choose the method that works best for you. We remember things that stand out in some way special to ourselves. Have a dip into some specialist books, look at various systems and work out one to suit you.

These are some of the more common ways to memorise. They all work extremely effectively.

➤ Make up a story in which each item appears. Telling the story triggers the items.

➤ Play with the initials, make a word, or words, from them perhaps. (There are no vowels in this example, but you could add some in.) Each initial triggers the word it represents.

➤ Use a form of code, a set of "memory hooks" on which anything can be hung. (See "Use Your Head" by Tony Buzan, for a full explanation.)

➤ Some people have visual memories and make a mental picture of the items, or of the actual shopping list. (This "eidetic memory" tends to be less common in adults than in children.)

➤ Reduce the list from ten to five by joining items into pairs (bread and butter, chewing gum and chocolate, etc).

These methods all have one thing in common. They require you to work with the material, to transform it in some way. To personalise it.

This not only personalises the material, it also ensures that you maximise the involvement of your senses since you have to *really* take in the data to process it. Then you have to draw it out from your short term memory, examine it, perhaps process it some more, and then hook it and store it in your long term memory. Very different from simple data input, done once only, in a form that someone else prefers!

The technique for the shopping list, using the "reduce to five method":

First, sort the list into a logic that works for you:

bread, butter, chewing gum, chocolate, kitchen roll, matches, pickles, salad cream, sardines, tea bags.

This gives:

> B & B, CG & C, KR & M, P & S, TSB. (Only five to remember.)

My personal logic says:

> B & B (go together obviously)
> CG & C (see one in shop and the other will be triggered)
> KR & M (paper burns)
> P & S (similar products, hardest to remember)
> TSB (the bank for me*)

(*TSB is a very well known British bank.)

The overall trigger is the store one walks past on the way in to work, when you should mentally note "no lunch before shopping".

Does that make sense to *you?* Not necessarily the logic, but the principle?

The technique is simple (but it involves work so the brain takes notice):

> ▶ Reduce the material to manageable proportions; a span of five

is good for most people. Use pencil and paper (to make a permanent record and to utilise as many of your senses as possible).

➤ Turn the material around so that it belongs to *you,* so that it becomes *your* list.

➤ Set it up so that it fits *your* mind.

➤ Talk it through several times to yourself; write it down on a fresh piece of paper; only go back to *your* original list if you have to — *never go back to the original.*

➤ Forget about it for an hour, then dig it out of the mind and say it over. Go back to your list if you have to.

➤ Go over it again as you go to bed. And again when you wake up.

➤ Once more rehearse it on the train (write it in the margin of your newspaper) and again as you pass the supermarket, then at coffee break.

This method uses "recall and review". (This is dealt with in more detail in Chapter 4.) Its use is exaggerated here. A short shopping list wouldn't justify so much time and effort, but as a principle does it make sense to you? Do you see the value? Would it work for you?

Final point — after the shopping is over the list will (usually) disappear from your mind because it is no longer important.

You can, of course, apply exactly the same principles to learning for an exam. Deposit basic data into your mental bank, draw it out in the exam room, and forget it within hours.(Beware! Examiners want more than simple recall of data, and it takes practice to develop your memory.)

Qualify in Management

You must practise sorting data into memorable pieces, and putting them in and out of your mind. There is no avoiding this, but you will find that you can be selective about what you need to memorise in this way. (This will be covered in Chapter 17.)

SUMMARY

- To memorise something takes effort.
- Memory works through the use of triggers and hooks.
- We remember what we want to remember.
- We remember that which we believe is important.
- We remember despite ourselves if the trigger is sufficiently powerful.
- Something put into our memory with care will stay.
- Use as many senses as possible to improve memory.
- Package material into pieces small enough to handle.
- Set up triggers — use exaggerated, absurd, coloured, imaginative symbols.
- Recognition is a powerful, automatic process, but we need to provide the triggers and hooks to make it work.
- *Recall* and *review* your memories.
- We must *understand* and *use* to recall effectively.
- Once the usefulness of some information is gone, we "forget" it.
- The depth of the mind is quite staggering: we surprise ourselves how we can dredge up pieces of "long forgotten" information.

USE *YOUR* BRAIN THE WAY THAT IS BEST FOR *YOU*.

Chapter 4
Learning

It may seem odd to look at learning after memory, but it has been done with a purpose. Almost anyone can memorise almost anything: if you were asked to remember a complicated chemical formula and there was a reward for getting it right, you'd probably work at it — and succeed.

But this wouldn't make you a chemist, nor would you actually know what it was you were carrying around in your head.

There is a great difference between memorising something and being able to use it. The difference is that to use it you have to learn it. To learn it you have to understand it. Understanding gives one a control over the material. Memory does not.

A simple definition is that:

Learning is demonstrated through a change in behaviour.

In other words, we only know that someone has truly learned when we see them putting that learning to use. Knowledge for its own sake really is pretty useless. (Management students have to demonstrate — to show — that they understand *and can use* the material covered on the course.)

There are three aspects to Learning that you must fully understand.

ATTITUDE

Attitude is crucial to success in learning. Unless you want to learn there is very little to be done about it. Can you be forced to learn? Can you?

You can be forced to sit in a classroom or forced to sit in front of a textbook; you can force yourself to do these things. But you can't be forced to learn, except by some kind of fear. Then you will learn the very minimum that you have to in order to avoid the punishment. This is not a very pleasant way to prepare for an examination.

You will find your unconscious mind a great help here. Once it knows that you have a problem that you consider important it will work away at it and will pop an answer up into your conscious mind, often when you are least expecting it. Cultivate this ability. Don't nag away at a problem. (We shall come back to this a little later.)

In Chapter 15 we cover the day of the exam. Here is a summary of what you will read on nervousness in that chapter:

It is natural to be nervous. Nerves can hinder, or help you.

Nerves are fear. Fear of the unknown, fear of failure, fear of looking silly.

The only person who should be frightened is the candidate who has done no proper preparation and that is really a fear of the aftermath — facing up to a fail.

Use "nerves" to your advantage. Channel them into heightened perception and an ability to concentrate and work for a longer stretch than is usual.

KNOWLEDGE

Knowledge is the basic material which must be stored, but not

necessarily in the memory. Very often it is a better use of your resources to know where to find what you need. (Rather than be good at spelling why not get a good dictionary and know how to use it properly? But, of course, you need a positive attitude towards the need for correct spelling if this is to work.)
Be careful here. You are aiming at passing and you can't spend too much time in the exam room looking up words in the dictionary. You will have to get the essential words sorted out between now and the exam.

Note that knowledge is of little or no value by itself.

What can you do with a head full of knowledge? Not much. You have to bring the knowledge out and put it to use. That means the right knowledge at the right time. Therefore you have to pack it away when you learn it so that you can find it again. Skills of recall and recognition are vital.

SKILL

Skill is the use of knowledge. For example, anyone can know how to type. It just takes a manual to be read, or for the system to be explained verbally. Then one knows about the QWERTY keyboard, about shift keys, about touch typing, etc.

But how many of those who *know* are also able to *do*. How long does it take a person to become a skilled typist? How does one define "skilled" anyway: 40 words per minute? 60? 80? 100?

It takes, on average, about 100 hours work for an interested person to reach a competent level of 40 wpm. Many more hours are needed to reach the higher speeds and it takes constant practice to sustain speed and accuracy. (Speed and accuracy are essential in a good typist. Both are skills, based on knowledge. But the overriding need is for a positive attitude.)

The *Double U* principle is very effective. Understanding and use are both needed if true learning is to be achieved. One mature student related the following anecdote about his learning. See how important attitude, understanding and use were to him.

My worst ever learning experience was the study of statistics for a post-graduate qualification. I hate statistics — no that's not true, I actually hate the calculations that are necessary. Anyway, I had to pass. I wanted to pass. I was going to pass.

So I had to sort out my attitude. Others could do it, others liked stats. So I decided that I would like statistics. Put a sign up over my desk — "Mike loves statistics". Wife and son soon began telling me how much I loved statistics. It became a joke and a total focus for about a month. During this time I slogged away at exercises, getting the feel of the numbers and the formulae. I managed a minimum of understanding, but gosh could I calculate!

I passed — and promptly switched back to my previous attitude. Now when I need statistics calculated I go to one of my colleagues at work and beg assistance. But at least I do know the value of statistics, I know their limitations, and I can see when someone is throwing numbers around without understanding them. That's all I need, thank you.

Understanding without *use* is of little value.

***Use* without *understanding* can be dangerous! *Both* are necessary.**

Let's jump ahead for a brief moment, to consider exam technique. What is it that examiners are actually looking for?

    100% knowledge of their subject?   — no!

    100% knowledge of their question paper?   — no!

    100% knowledge of the questions you answer? — no!

All they actually ask is that the candidate answers the required number of questions *and* gets a pass mark (usually a minimum of

50%). So no candidate ever has to show knowledge of the whole subject.

If this is so, *and it is,* it opens up three interesting points:

1. There should be some way of forecasting the most probable areas in which questions will be set.
2. There should be some way to *ignore* areas of the syllabus!
3. If 1 and 2 are correct it is possible to minimise the workload whilst retaining a high probability of success.

One very strong argument for continuous assessment rather than an end of course exam is based upon exactly this point. If learning is important, and it is, then passing an exam does not prove that a student really knows the subject. Well managed continuous assessment monitors learning throughout a long period and uses a variety of assessment methods. This is a more rounded way to evaluate a student's level of achievement.

Once the workload has been reduced and the probability of success has been determined, then *you* can concentrate your efforts. (The fourth section of this book is all about techniques to pass exams — but don't try to get there too soon.)

Back to Learning...

Are we agreed that *you* really cannot be forced to learn? That fear is not very motivational? Hopefully we are.

The point now becomes — what is motivational. What is **motivation.**

Motivation is a feeling, a striving, that is internal. You have a range of motivations covering all aspects of your life. In each you can place yourself on a scale running from highly motivated to de-motivated. Remember the student working for a statistics exam? He was highly motivated and took positive action to channel that motivation through himself and his family so as to give him a charge of energy at the time he needed it.

Motivation is almost always linked with **incentive**. An incentive is something external, a reward of some kind. It is necessary to match the correct incentive(s) to the motivational needs of an individual.

What incentives do *you* respond to? Which items on this list apply to *you?* Can you extend the list?

Basic survival	Happiness
Curiosity	Creativity
Challenge	Competition/Rivalry
Ambition	Achievement
Pride in self	Pleasure in system and order
Pride in group	Money

If you ticked money as an incentive, please think again. Is it really money that is the incentive? Or is it what you can do with the money?

For instance, if you were given £200 perhaps you would buy a new tennis racket but your friend would add to his record collection. Your mother might put it into her holiday fund; your father might buy a new suit.

It is the same £200, but we would use it differently; the actual incentive is not the money itself. What would you use the £200 for? How many who read this book would actually keep 200 £1 coins at home just to look at?

Now relate what you know about incentive and motivation to *yourself* and *your* exams. What are the incentives for you to pass? Which is the most important? Why are you taking the examinations? What will you gain? Is it all worth it? Why?

Stop. Read the last paragraph again. It is very important for you to understand exactly why you are taking the exams.

WHY ARE YOU TAKING THE COURSE?

Probably you haven't thought the problem through before. Had it occurred to you that it could be a problem? This could be *the single most important section in the whole book*. Crack the motivation/incentive problem and you have a foundation of rock on which to build. When you are tired or when you have to choose between study and going out with friends, come back to:

(a) "What am I doing it for?"
(b) "Is the long-term benefit of passing better than the short-term alternative?"

So it is important for you to **write down** your incentives and motivations. Say, very clearly and shortly, exactly why you are doing the exam. Then put the notice up where you study and you will not fail to see it.

You won't be able, probably, to complete this analysis in a few minutes. It will take several days for you to work out exactly how you feel and to get it down in print, but it is worth it.

HOW DO WE LEARN?

Your combined senses (sight, sound, touch, taste, smell and your "sixth sense") combine to enable you to perceive, which is a pretty important thing to do. (Perception is the process of recognising or identifying something.)

We know that tucked away in our minds we have a whole series of experiences and a range of knowledge. We also process an incredible amount of new data every second of our lives. It is estimated that our sense organs are processing some 50,000,000 signals every waking second!

Thus we all develop an automatic sifter to discard that which is irrelevant. The term "sixth sense" is used partly to describe the automatic validation of data; but it is also a provider of data. It draws on our experiences and feeds up to our conscious mind. "Look out", it may say, "we have met this type of person before. Don't trust him!"

This internal source of data will colour our perception of the person we have just met, without our conscious knowledge! We may like to call this example "prejudice", but it comes from our sub-conscious, from our internal store of data, and so it affects our perception. We can't ignore it.

If we can't ignore it, then we should ensure that we control it. We can become aware that we are feeding ourselves data and actively test that data in the present situation. Is it reliable or valuable? Has it been triggered in error because the situation is similar but not identical?

There is a scene in "The Cruel Sea" where a new Australian lieutenant has a hard time simply because a year before another Australian officer had been most unpleasant. The lesson had been learned — Australians are bad news! Of course they aren't all bad, but it took a while for the characters to sort this out for themselves.

Be aware of your own sixth sense. Learn to listen to it but check what it is saying — especially about examinations. Probably you will find a whole mess and muddle of nasty impressions; do try to put them into perspective.

Examinations can be *fun* — really!

USE OF OUR SENSES

Can we agree that *sight* is by far the most important of our five physical senses. Let us hope so, because it undoubtedly is.

It is important to you in the classroom, because you will be listening to your tutor with *your eyes* as well as your ears. Every time we listen to someone we watch the body language that accompanies speech.

Sometimes it reinforces and strengthens what is being said; sometimes it cancels it for us — "Don't believe a word of it" the body says. We tend to take more notice of the body language than the oral message, sight is so very powerful!

Have you ever been to a film where the sound is just a *fraction* out of synchronization? Then you know how uncomfortable that makes one feel.

In the classroom there is the need to read what goes on the board or the overhead projector, to read handouts and to read what one has written as notes.

In private study sight continues to be the most important sense and in the exam room it is certainly your main means of communication with the examiner. He or she must read what you write. For the examiner the primary contact with you is by sight. (In Chapter 19 we come back to this point.)

So, it is extremely important to use sight to its maximum effect:

1. Take notes when learning. From a tutor or from a text. These notes are *yours*, your version of the material given to you to master.

   In the process of taking notes consider what happens — you see/hear some material. Your sense organs present it as part of the 50 million signals, and your automatic sifter allows the material through. You accept this into the short term memory and immediately determine which elements of it to put into your notes.

   Then you create the necessary signals and transmit them to your arm, hand and fingers. They carry out the writing for you, whilst you are also engaged in processing the next data input and checking that you are writing what you intended to write.

   It is all very complex, and it is happening at an incredible rate.

It is no wonder that students come out of a lesson with notes but no actual recall of the lesson content in any detail.

2. It follows from 1 that the notes must be clear and that they need to be re-written rather quickly.

Mind mapping the classroom or textbook notes is an excellent idea. It takes practice, but once mastered saves an incredible amount of time. Most importantly it also ensures that each page of notes is unique. Each will have its own shape and individuality.

Thus each will be easier to remember, since you will find that you will be able to use your sixth sense to "see" your notes. You cannot do this if all your notes are identical in style!

Re-write your notes and simplify them at the same time, about 24 hours after they were first taken. *This is the time to get them ready for your end-of-course revision.*

3. Use colours to add interest and to highlight topic areas. Add sketches, cartoons, diagrams to make your notes memorable and to provide triggers and hooks.

4. In the exam room sight is vital. It is your main communication link with the examiner, so plan its use well.

Present your material in an interesting way; don't be frightened of using some colour in your exam answers. Make your paper look attractive. Nothing is more boring than an examination answer book filled with line after line of essay — especially when the writing is bad and the pen blotchy!

Include diagrams, sketches, or whatever is appropriate. A picture *does* save a 1000 words, but you'd be surprised how few are used in exam answers when so many could be!

THE IMPORTANCE OF PHYSICAL EXERCISE

It is very important to schedule both mental and physical activity into your learning. The mind needs time to assimilate and process new data, and the body needs to rid itself of the physical and mental tension that builds up during concentrated periods of study.

Research indicates quite clearly that more learning takes place if the periods of study are brief and are interspersed with physical activity.

An effective break can be as short as five minutes, but it must be taken outside the study area; preferably in the fresh air. It must certainly involve a physical stretching, perhaps a short walk.

REVIEW AIDS EFFECTIVE MEMORY

Tony Buzan suggests that if you don't regularly revise your work you will forget most of it very quickly. You have to impress your subconscious mind with the importance of the material and then keep reminding it of the need to keep it stored and accessible.

It may seem like hard work, but you really only have to glance over your notes. If they are set up with good triggers and you understand the material you will really get to know your notes very quickly. And you will be able to recall them in the exam room.

Studies show that properly spaced review, as a part of planned learning, can keep recall constantly high.

Note that athletes warm up before their events. They need to have their muscles not only warmed up and loose, but also rehearsed in the moves they will be making in the event. Sprinters practise starts, when they are warm; soccer players practise shooting into goal; goalkeepers "get their eye in".

Students who warm up their minds before a period of study are better able to learn. So a quick look through past notes immediately before

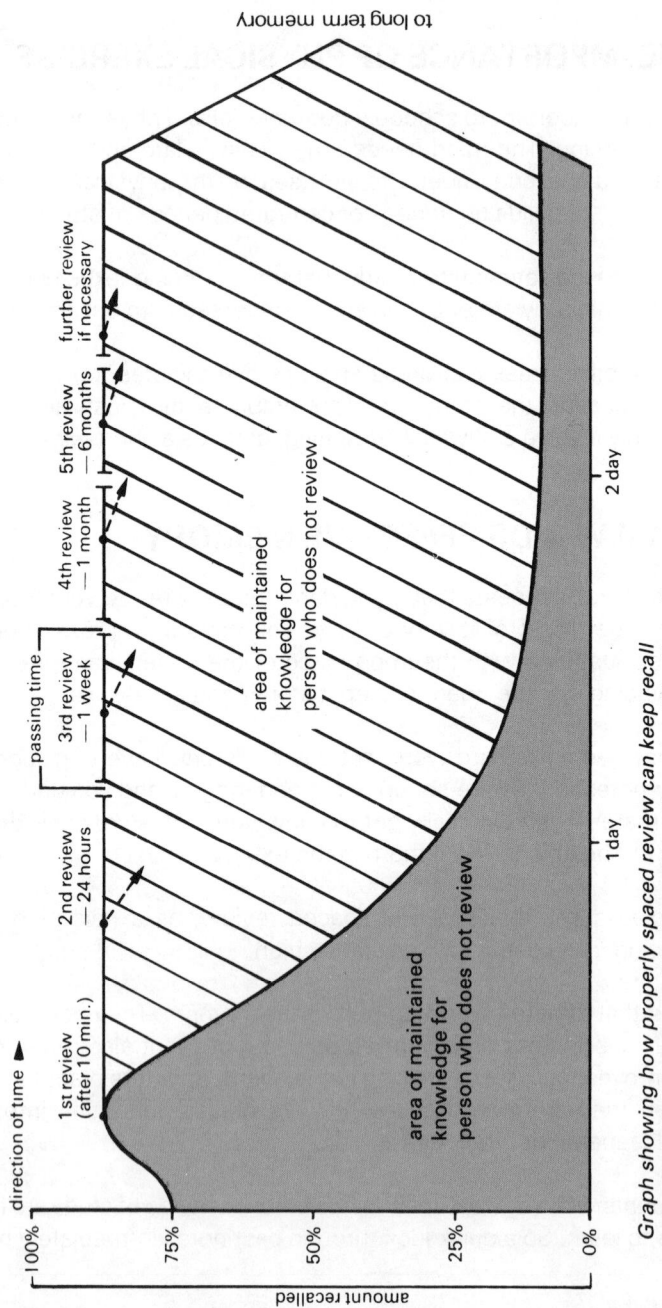

Graph showing how properly spaced review can keep recall constantly high (see page 59). (From "Use Your Head" by Tony Buzan, BBC. Reproduced by permission.)

each study time can only help — but *you* have to plan it into your schedule. (This also ensures that your brain is alerted as to where you want the new data stored.)

THE THEORY OF LEARNING

Much work has been done on learning theory, but you don't need to delve deeply (unless you get hooked on the subject, and do it for fun).

What you do need to fully *understand* is that what most people call "learning" is actually only memory. Revision, if it involves sitting reading and re-reading textbooks and notes, is of very little value to most people.

Learning is actually understanding and use. There is no substitute. You have to choose between a thorough knowledge of your subject and a sufficient knowledge to get you through your course.

Start by examining the structure and purpose of your course — that will help direct your learning effort. We shall return to the importance of each subject and the allocation of your priorities later in the book.

Here are three final points:

1. It is a definite fact that some learning comes together in a rush. You struggle along, feel totally lost, then suddenly "the penny drops" — "ah ha!" you say, "got it". We presume that the unconscious is working away at the problem and that the last connection is suddenly made and the whole thing makes sense. *(The Gestalt principle.)*

   So don't stop working on a tough subject, but do try to look at it from several different angles. It is *not* cheating to look up a solution to a problem and then work back from it to the question. It is *silly* to do that, however, and then not work the example through from the front. Work one or two more as well, to be sure you have (finally) cracked it.

2. Learn by association. Be sure to set up associative triggers that are brash, colourful, unusual. Help your mind to help you.

3. You will often learn as much from a fellow student as from the tutor. Perhaps the student has a feeling for the subject, as you will have for another subject. Perhaps the student gets on better with the tutor than you do. Why worry? Don't ignore a valuable source of learning aid.

SUMMARY

- Learning is *not* memory — it is memory plus understanding.
- Effective memory is the ability to recall data when needed.
- Understanding is best achieved through *use*.
- Attitude is crucial to success.
- Knowledge is necessary, before skill is developed.
- We forget very quickly, unless we work on remembering.
- Link incentives to motivations. *Write down your own!*
- Break learning into small pieces, within your personal span.
- Use all your senses.
- Use your unconscious mind — allow a problem to brew away in there.
- Practise recall and review.
- Set up hooks and triggers. (Learn by association.)
- Train your mind to automatic, skilled, learning *that works for you*.

DO IT YOUR WAY — but DO IT.

Chapter 5
Study Skills

There are essential key points to successful study. They are outlined in this chapter, but you need to read wider and to experiment, so that you select the method that works best for you. (You will find that some points in this chapter are repeats of material already covered. This is deliberate since this chapter is intended to pull together the key elements of study skills without explaining why each element is important. Every element is explained elsewhere in the book.)

PRIORITIES

Get your priorities right. Courses must be passed, but there is a full life to lead too! The only way is to build your studies into your normal life. They must become a part of it. They cannot be tacked on; they must be absorbed into it.

Motivation is crucial to success. As soon as you hear yourself say "Not today" stop and very closely question whether you are dodging out. And if so, why?

Don't expect too much of yourself. Set limits, organise your time, plan what you can do in advance and monitor your progress against plan.

If you feel a subject is "getting away from you" take action at once. Usually you will need outside help. Talk with anyone who can see the problem from a different perspective. Often talking a problem through will enable you to solve it for yourself.

INDIVIDUALITY

All learning is individual. Some people will study the way you do, others very differently. It doesn't matter. Seek the techniques that are effective for you.

Set aside specific times for study each week. That is not hard. The hard part is keeping to your self-selected programme.

OBJECTIVES

The best way to achieve your overall objective at the end of the course is to continually set yourself "Sub-objectives". The whole thing is too big to handle, therefore break it up into bits and the problem comes into perspective.

An example from sport is that it is too much to go out to win a tennis match, although that is the overall objective. The successful player takes it game by game, even playing "one point at a time".

FACTORS WHICH AFFECT LEARNING

Organisation

Lack of organisation will retard your rate of learning.

Plateaux

Learning "plateaux" are simply "flat spots" where you feel that no progress is being made. They are common to everyone and cannot be avoided. Your motivation will see you through providing you are expecting them and don't panic.

Attention

Everyone's attention wanders after a time. The time can be as little as seven or eight minutes, up to a maximum of about 40 minutes. Many students try to concentrate for too long at a time. It is best to break up the work, schedule physical activity breaks and breaks for refreshments.

Understanding

You *must* understand the material. Understanding comes through use.

Revision/review

Frequent review is necessary to aid memory. Using your knowledge is the best revision possible.

Involvement

Active involvement consolidates learning. Do your assignments, discuss your learning with friends. Teach somebody else: there is no finer way to learn a subject than to have to teach it.

Interest

Learning without interest is sterile and very difficult. There is a good reason why a topic has to be learned, find out what it is, why you have to learn it. Decide if it has value for you. If not, drop it! Then you can stop worrying about it. Don't be half-baked about study. You can't study without interest.

Interference

Previous knowledge may "interfere" with learning. Perhaps what you are being taught appears to interfere with what you already know or believe? You must sort this problem out if it occurs. Don't be passive about it. Research, test and decide what is correct, for you.

Flexibility

Be flexible. If one method of learning fails, try another.

TEXTBOOKS

You are probably conditioned to read a book from front to back. You have probably read this book line by line. Fine, this is a workbook where the structure is designed in the knowledge that most people will work from front to back. But textbooks are not like that.

A textbook is not a novel where the narrative unfolds and you don't want to know the development of the story ahead of time. A textbook is for reference, for research and for dipping into for specific help.

Often you need to see how a problem is resolved as an aid to your learning. It can help you to understand the logic of the solution. It is *not* cheating to approach a problem from front, back or side; from above and below. All that matters is that you truly understand and that you learn.

Texts and correspondence school notes are fine, but they all suffer from the same complaint. They are static. They are fixed and unchanging. So if you don't understand today, you are not likely to understand tomorrow. You have to overcome this problem.

Get into a book by not treating it with any particular respect. Pick it up, weigh it in your hand, look at it. Does it feel right? Does it feel difficult? (It sound silly, but try it anyway.) Then open it at the back and look through the index. Do the terms mean anything to you? How many have you come across before? Thumb through quickly; are there any pictures? Any diagrams? Any anecdotes? Is the text solid print? Does it look too heavy, or too simple? How do you feel about it?

Dip into a couple of chapter summaries. If there are none, what does this tell you about the author? How do you feel about the book? Look at the table of contents, dip into the preface.

In short, get a an overview of the material; get the newness and the mystery out of the book. Make if yours — if you want it. (If you can do this in a bookshop it will greatly help your choice of text. If it is a set text then you have to master it before it masters you.)

When you have a feel for a textbook you shouldn't have to read every word. Take what you need from a book. No more, and no less.

Do not mishandle textbooks, but do be firmly in control of them. They are tools to be worked with.

If a book is yours don't hesitate to write in it, to highlight sections, to add your own comments. If you have to look up a definition be sure to write it into the margin of the text so you don't have to look it up ever again. (If the book is not yours *never* write in it, use slips of paper between the pages instead.)

An author is putting forward his or her view. Look for other books on the subject. You will often be pleasantly surprised to find that eminent people disagree on the same subject. You are then free to associate yourself with the one that most clearly represents your view. You are also able to contrast the views in your examination answers and show the examiner that you are widely read.

STUDY PLAN

Maximise your learning and ensure that you get full value for every minute that you devote to study. This means that you *must* have a study plan. A method that works very well is "SQ3R".

SQ3R

Survey — Take a quick look at the main details of the material you intend to study, a chapter from a textbook, or a section of a correspondence course. *Don't* try too much at one time.

Question — Work out your own questions — what you need to know from the material.

Read — Read the material in the usual way, but actively look for the main topic(s).

Recall — Go back through the material and make notes on the important points (take as many as possible from your head, but check them against the material).

Review — Check that you have answered the questions that you set for yourself and that your notes are accurate and memorable.

Learning from written material *must* be active. You must work *on it* and *with it* to achieve understanding.

NOTE MAKING

Select — Do not copy every word. Reserve this for the special times when you need a quote.

— Note only the main points, with subsidiary points where you will find them helpful.

— Include references in your notes (eg the book title and author), especially when consolidating notes from several sources.

Abbreviate	— Work to your own shorthand. If "mkt" means market, then "mkting" means marketing. "M" or "mt" can be used for management and so on. Be consistent.
Underline	— Headings and main points. The use of colour is highly recommended; but don't make your notes look like a rainbow.
Style	— Lists of points can *sometimes* be useful.
	— Use your own words, except when noting a quotation.
	— Write clearly. Notes you cannot read are useless.
	— Make your notes distinctive. (Mind mapping is a very good technique that you should master.)
Leave space	— Don't squash notes. Give them space, make them easier to read. (This also allows you to add notes as your studies progress.)
Revise/review	— Keep in touch with your learning, keep it fresh.
	— Compare your old notes with the work you are doing later and amend as necessary.
Simplify	— Notes are intended to simplify your learning. They should be abstracts of your learning; they should act as triggers for your memory. Therefore they should be simple and memorable.

SUMMARY

- Build your studies into your life. Set priorities.
- Find out your own *individual* learning style — then keep to it.
- Set clear, attainable, sub--objectives.
- Expect the learning plateaux and don't be discouraged.
- Work to discover, then increase, your span of attention.
- You *must* understand if you are to learn effectively.
- Review and revise regularly.
- Previous knowledge must not interfere with new learning.
- Treat textbooks as tools. It is not necessary to read a text from cover to cover.
- Write in *your* books if this helps you to learn.
- SQ3R — Survey, Question, Read, Recall, Review.
- Make your notes so that they help your mind remember.
- Use your own words in notes, except for direct quotes.
- Leave space in notes; they are then easier to read and there is room to add to them later.

TAKE RESPONSIBILITY FOR YOUR OWN LEARNING.

Section Two

The Task You Face

Qualify in Management

The term "centre" is used throughout this book to avoid the clumsy and time consuming "college or polytechnic". "Centre" should be taken to include any form of study, involving a tutor, by which you elect to take your course.

Chapter 6
Management and Management Courses

MANAGEMENT

"Management" is a term that is used very casually throughout industry and commerce. What does it mean?

There are specific definitions of "management" and many styles of management. What they come down to, in essence, is that management is the *achievement of results through people*. Thus, managers are found in every functional area of an organisation. Managers of personnel, of finance, of production, of marketing all need technical subject skills, but general management ability is what makes managers really effective.

A person with an excellent command of balance sheets, profit and loss accounts and cash flow projections may not be able to manage a team of people. The *Peter Principle* says that people are promoted to the level of their own incompetence. (Being successful in a series of ever more senior jobs does not guarantee success in the next step up.)

It is also argued that the more successful a person is in a technical or functional capacity the less likely he or she is to be able to manage others. The best sales representative does not make the best sales manager; the best teacher does not make the best school head; the best mechanic is unlikely to be the best workshop foreman. There are management skills to be learned. From these comes the ability to achieve results through the motivation, leadership and control of others.

A good manager can transfer across functions. A functional specialist cannot make the same move. It is for you to study the various theories of management but if you agree with the basic hypothesis it follows that a sales manager can move to manage an office in central administration, then a personnel section, on to a marketing department, then to research and development and up to the board of directors.

In each job he or she will need to know only the basics about how individual jobs are done but a lot about how people are motivated and led. The good generalist manager needs to know what can be expected of a functional specialist. He or she must know what questions to ask and when a piece of work is up to the required standard. There is no need to know *how* to do it, but it is vital to know that it is being done efficiently and effectively.

A course for managers will, therefore, take the principles of management as a major element but also provide sufficient knowledge and skills in functional areas to enable the manager to appreciate the potentials — both positive and negative — in each area. You won't get through a management course without study in each of the major areas commonly found in industry and commerce but you will not need individual subject knowledge in depth.

Obviously, everyone starts somewhere and you will have come to management from an individual functional area. You may be trained as a chef or as an accounts clerk. You may be in a sales force or be a trained nurse. Naturally you will bring to management the elements of your own personality that made you select your starting point in the first place and you will also apply your own unique perspective to management which will be coloured by your experiences.

MANAGEMENT COURSES

To those testing general management knowledge and skills it seems obvious that individuality of style and approach is necessary and unavoidable. Each manager is different and each manager's style is special to him or to her. That is not important. What is important is that the individuals each realise the effect of their management styles. And the necessary actions that must follow certain management styles. (An autocratic manager, for example, would be unwise to try to build a team that felt it must debate and achieve consensus before taking action. There would be clashes. Very quickly!)

It is important, therefore, for you to show your assessors that you have an understanding of management theories and that you have made a personal judgement about your management style and the knock-on effects that you will have to deal with.

It is also important for you to show that you have mastered the basics in each of the functional areas.

Finally, you have to show that you understand and can deal with the cross-functional interfaces. That means you must be aware of the styles, abilities, requirements and expectations of specialists in other functions; and be able to communicate effectively.

The two management courses providing a focus for this book are the NEBSM Certificate and the BTEC Certificate in Management Studies (CMS). The general principles apply to all management courses that are assessed by continuous assessment and so the examples chosen apply across a range of courses.

You will find that either the NEBSM or the CMS course has been specified when examples are used in this book. "NEBSM or CMS" is unnecessarily confusing and the principles of each example apply equally to both courses.

You should, therefore, read the book taking each example as applying to your course — even if you are not taking NEBSM or CMS.

GENERAL PRINCIPLES

Whatever course you are taking there are general principles that apply:

1. **Discover your course structure**

    How is your workload programmed? You will find that there is a structure to the course programme and that if you keep to the schedule you will not be overworked. It is common for a student to allow course work to build up until he or she is overwhelmed.

    In particular, the project can suffer very badly through insufficient time being found for it early in the programme.

    It is your responsibility to see that you manage your time. You must not expect your tutors to manage it for you.

2. **Identify the assessment scheme**

    How are the grades or marks awarded across the course? You must know, so that you can schedule your workload appropriately. There is no secret schedule, you can be told. Be certain to ask your tutor. Once you know, be sure to allocate your effort so that you achieve a satisfactory grade or pass mark *as a minimum* in each element of the course. (See Chapter 7.)

3. **Open a course planning diary**

    Ensure that you have entered the dates for assignments, project reviews and completion, residential weekend(s), written and oral exams, etc. Monitor your progress. Discipline yourself. (See Chapter 11.)

4. **Set up a "buddy system"**

    Agree with two other course members that you will "buddy up". Then the team ensures that any absent member is provided with course material, is alerted to changes in dates or special activities scheduled by the tutor or by the class (parties!).

Often you will find that when you don't quite understand a topic one of your buddies will. If not, there are still three of you to work on the problem and that is a lot better than struggling alone!

5. **Assume help is available**

    Your tutors are motivated to help students pass. (We cover this in more detail in Chapter 8.) They do not want you to struggle unaided.

    Tutors respond to students who think through their problems and arrange to see them with some advance warning. They are likely to be less willing if you are muddled in what you want and if you expect instant attention. (The tutor has a daily schedule too, and another class to attend after he or she leaves yours.)

6. **Do not read textbooks**

    We covered this in Chapter 5, but it is important to re-state the fact that texts are tools for the student. They should be used for a specific purpose, at a specific time. For example, as a research aid when completing an assignment or the day before a lesson on a particular topic so that you are at least slightly familiar with what is to come. You will find the ways that work best for you. Don't expect to learn by simply reading a text!

National Examinations Board for Supervisory Management (NEBSM)

Until January 1989, this body was known as the National Examinations Board for Supervisory Studies (NEBSS). The concept that supervisors were in some way different from management, that there were employees, supervisors and managers, is now dead (or at least dying fast). It is now recognised that supervisors are *first line management,* and the NEBSM has changed its title to accommodate this fact.

(You will examine the concept of first line management and you will discover that it is not by title that one is judged. Many with the title "manager" are no more than line supervisors, with little executive authority or responsibility.)

NEBSM is an independent body, established in 1964 by Government, with the remit to "further the Education and Training of Supervisors to enable them to discharge their duties confidently and effectively". NEBSM is recognised as setting high standards in the education of first line managers who have little or no formal academic background. NEBSM offers awards at three levels: Introductory, Certificate and Diploma.

The NEBSM Certificate is an acceptable entry qualification to courses of study at higher levels of management training (such as the BTEC Certificate in Management Studies). It is by far the most popular NEBSM qualification (with some 14,000 students taking it each year). In this book we shall concentrate upon the Certificate course.

NEBSM believe *"that the supervisor is the key front line manager — the person who can 'make or break' top management plans. The trained supervisor is the person who has the skills to make Senior Managers' decisions work in practice"*.

Note: There is considerable emphasis placed upon training and upon the use of skills. Education is important, but skill development is seen as crucial.

NEBSM standards *"are monitored by a team of Assessors appointed by the Board by virtue of their interest in supervisory management education and training, together with their personal experience of management"*.

Note: Selection and monitoring of assessors is very carefully controlled. NEBSM recognise that the quality of their qualifications depends very much upon individual centres which offer the courses achieving a consistency of quality. The reputation of a NEBSM Certificate depends, ultimately, upon the quality of the assessors and the system under which they are managed.

THE CERTIFICATE COURSE

NEBSM Certificate Courses are built to meet the needs of identified students in specific areas of work. The content is designed to equip the supervisors on the course to do their jobs better, and to prepare them for career advancement.

Thus no two NEBSM courses are likely to be the same. (It is very important, therefore, for *you* to find out exactly how *your* course is structured.)

There will be a common framework, however. A NEBSM Certificate will be built around five themes. The themes and the most likely sub-headings within each are:

1. **Principles and practice of supervisory management**

    Needs and rewards

    Enriching work

    Workteams

    Team leading

    Leading change

    Organisation systems

    Supervising in the system

    Supervising with authority

    Taking decisions

2. **Technical aspects of supervision**

    Looking at figures

    Using graphs

    Method study

Easy statistics
Quality control
Controlling output
Value analysis
Quality circles
Computers
Stores control
Managing time
Descriptive statistics
Supervisors and marketing

3. **Communication**
Communicating
Speaking skills
Writing skills
Communication systems
Orders and instructions
Project preparation

4. **Economic and financial aspects**
Accounting for money
Control via budgets
Cost reduction
Wage payment systems
The national economy
Cost centres

5. **Industrial relations**

   Training plans

   Training sessions

   Discipline and the law

   Health and safety

   Industrial relations in action

   Equality at work

   Hiring people

   Supervising and the law.

(The above comprises the NEBSM SuperSeries of Open Learning packs. A course based in a college or other approved centre will work to the same main headings but adjust the content of each to meet the needs of the students for whom the course is designed. Thus, a course for retail supervisors will have a module on consumer law that would not be needed by production supervisors. Equally, method study may be inappropriate for retail but vital for production managers.)

The shape of the course

Courses vary in shape to fit the needs of the students and their employers. It is unusual, however, to find a NEBSM Certificate course that does not extend over several months with the students attending on some form of release from work. The course may be "blocked" into weeks but more usually it is set up on a one day per week basis. Thus the students have the opportunity to put into practice what they are learning, and to bring actual situations into the classroom. A NEBSM course should deal with theory in the context of what is actually happening. (Remember that the NEBSM has a strong inclination towards skill development.)

The content of each of the five headings will be structured so that it comes to the students in a balanced way. You will not receive all the content of one section before moving on to the next. There will also be considerable cross-referencing between the headings. (The only reason they are set out so distinctly is to enable the planners to structure a course so that nothing is omitted and that material is presented to students in an order that helps them learn.)

A **project** and a **residential weekend** will usually be part of a Certificate course. Both are covered later in the book (Chapters 12 and 13). For now it is sufficient to say that they are there to help students to understand what they are learning. The project is only a problem if it is made into one, by the student usually. The residential weekend is always fun, even though it is common for students to be a little concerned about it in advance. We shall look in detail at both of these important areas.

BUSINESS AND TECHNICIAN EDUCATION COUNCIL (BTEC)
CERTIFICATE IN MANAGEMENT STUDIES (CMS)

The Business and Technician Education Council came into existence in 1983 as an amalgamation of the Business Education Council and the Technician Education Council (BEC and TEC). It exists *"to advance the quality and availability of work-related education for those in, or preparing for, employment"*. The fundamental aim of the Council is *"that students on BTEC courses develop the necessary competence in their careers in their own, employers' and national interest"*.

Note that BTEC is concerned with "competence", the skills of the job; and that it is student centred. BTEC courses are designed with student needs primarily in mind. Equipping students to meet the needs of the employers is central to BTEC philosophy. It follows that a CMS will be designed with the needs of the students at the forefront, but with considerable concern for the needs of employers — usually employers local to the centre.

The CMS is suitable for mangers in all sectors of the economy, but is

Management and Management Courses

aimed at those in an early stage of their development as managers, especially those who have experience in working as supervisors. It follows that many who complete a NEBSM Certificate go on to take a CMS.

To get the most from a CMS managers must practise their skills at work: the CMS is primarily aimed at those in employment. It can be offered in many forms, but the most common is day release where students attend one day a week for an academic year. (A total of 300 hours of instruction is required.) A residential period of two or three days is normally required as part of the course.

To enrol for a CMS applicants must fulfil minimum entry requirements. They should:

(a) have acquired and/or be acquiring experience in a management role;

(b) have at least three years' experience in a responsible position;

(c) hold a BTEC National Certificate or Diploma, or demonstrate equivalent attainment.

Tutors are instructed to select applicants on their ability to contribute to and successfully complete the course. In doing this they may, exceptionally, admit applicants who do not meet the minimum entry requirements. (They have to identify, in advance, the criteria they will use in making such exceptions.)

Each CMS course is designed by the centre providing it, to best suit the needs of particular managers and their employees. National control of standards is maintained by BTEC through clear policy guidelines and validation, moderation and monitoring systems.

There is no fixed content for a CMS, nor is there any fixed method of assessment, but BTEC must approve the detailed plans for each proposed CMS, in advance. Without prior validation by BTEC, the course cannot run.

BTEC provide a guide to the groups of management competencies that managers are likely to need and which are likely to be included in a CMS.

They specify that this is not definitive and that it is for centres to determine content in the light of local need. The BTEC groups of competencies are:

1. **Human resource management**

    Interpersonal skills; communication skills; managing group processes; team building; leadership; motivation; delegation; managing relationships; managing stress; evaluating performance; developing others; resolving conflict; political awareness.

2. **Decision making**

    Establishing objectives; information handling; creativity; logical thinking; perceptual skills; deciding priorities; using diagnostic concepts — eg quantitative analysis and financial indicators; considering the impact of decisions.

3. **Resource management**

    Financial control - eg making and controlling budgets; identifying the financial impact of decisions; entrepreneurial skills; using information technology; effective use of resources; commercial and legal awareness.

4. **Self-development**

    Self-analysis and self-assessment; learning skills; time management; self-confidence; flexibility; resilience.

Most of these areas of competence require a mixture of knowledge, appropriate attitudes and skills. It is expected that student learning will be encouraged through a correct balance of learning opportunities provided by the course team.

Management of a CMS will be the responsibility of a course team, probably of about three staff, who make a substantial commitment to the course, one of whom will be the course tutor (or course co-ordinator). There will be an examinations board to determine student results.

The examinations board must consist of:

(a) all who teach on the course;

(b) the continuing education moderator;

(c) the external advisor;

(d) a senior member of staff, as chairman.

CMS Course Tutors are required to pay particular attention to:

(a) **Sequencing** — activities should be progressive and decrease the dependence of students upon their tutors.

(b) **Transferability** — activities should help students to transfer their abilities to new problems and situations.

(c) **Relevance** — activities should be "real world" relevant. Senior line managers from course members' organisations should be used as an important source of information and assistance.

(d) **Integration** — realistic activities should demand the application of a range of knowledge and skills.

The award of the CMS to individual students is conditional upon each meeting the requirements of the assessment scheme. The examination board will evaluate overall results and grant either a pass, a referral, or a fail. (It is not expected that students recruited with integrity should fail.)

What, finally, is the difference between the NEBSM and the CMS? They cover much the same material, and have much the same duration. CMS students are, however, expected to work to a much greater depth, and to do it more quickly. If you go on from the CMS to the Diploma in Management Studies (the DMS) you will find that it lasts twice as long as the CMS and that the content comes at you almost twice as fast! (Or so it will seem until you learn to move faster.) Just as assignments are less pressured at the beginning of a course, compared to the end, so more senior courses demand faster response times, plus greater understanding.

SUMMARY

- Managers achieve results through people.

- Management is a skill in its own right.

- It is possible to develop management skills and to add them to specialist subject skills.

- Good managers manage across a range of specialist subject areas.

- Management courses help students to acquire knowledge, develop appropriate attitudes and practise the skills that are needed to succeed as a manager.

- Management students should:

    discover their course structure;

    identify the assessment scheme;

    maintain a course diary;

    set up a buddy system;

    assume help is available — and use it;

    use textbooks as tools.

SUCCESS COMES THROUGH SELF MANAGEMENT TO MEET THE NEEDS OF YOUR COURSE.

Chapter 7
Continuous Assessment Explained

GRADING

In this book "marks" are referred to, rather than "grades". This is because the grading system, where students are awarded a lettered grade (usually A-F) only disguises the fact that pieces of work are evaluated numerically!

Grading, where students are given a letter (or sometimes a number) to indicate the quality band of their work, is good in principle. In principle it is good to grade rather than mark; in principle it is good that almost everyone passes a course. But in the world outside education people believe that to pass a course with an A grade is better than to pass with an E. In fact employers ask for "O Level Grade C" or "CSE Grade 1".

The use of grades allows students to be grouped, but it also removes the necessity for tutors to indicate exactly how many marks have been awarded. It is sad that some students will argue that "John got 82% and I only got 80%" and then demand a detailed explanation. But, if healthy, this debate between student and tutor keeps both on their toes. Moving to a grading system does not solve the problem — perhaps it disguises it.

Under a grading system the results have to be processed numerically!

Thus every grade will be awarded a notional mark so that it can be entered into a computer. As soon as this is done every student in a grade appears to be equal. Thus the student who scrapes in with 61% is judged to be the same as one who achieved 74%!

If your course is graded, remember that underlying the grades is a numeric system. Many of your tutors will actually mark in numbers and then convert their percentage totals to the appropriate grade. If this sounds silly then perhaps you are not the only one to think so, and perhaps the system can be changed.

The CMS is awarded to all who pass. There are no grades of pass. Thus it becomes even more important for you to be able to show your boss, and future employers, the quality of *your* work on *your* CMS. The reputation of your centre will be known to personnel managers, and you will have a record of your personal achievement to show if you keep a personal development journal (see Chapter 11).

CONTINUOUS ASSESSMENT

Can we agree that there needs to be some way of measuring the success achieved by each student?

The purpose of study for most people is self-improvement. Self-improvement, by itself, is a very vague term. It is not possible for another person to know if an individual has "self-improved"; nor to know by how much. There has to be measurement; some yardstick against which to judge progress.

A reliable, valid and comparable assessment of progress and of achievement is needed. Examinations have traditionally been the way progress has been measured. How far do they measure up to the need for reliability, validity and comparability? What do the terms mean?

> **Reliability** means that an exam will produce a consistent score from one use to the next for the same individual or group. Also it

will produce consistent results when marked by different people.

Validity means that an exam achieves what the examiner intended it should. Does it cover the width and depth of the syllabus? Does it provide for qualitative and quantitative measurement? Does it provide accurate prediction (when allowing candidates through to a further year of study, for example).

Comparability means that the results of individuals taking different exams, or groups taking the same exam, can be compared. (All candidates taking A level French, for example, from every examining board should achieve results that are cross comparable. It should not matter which exam is taken, the result should be the same.)

It is extremely difficult for examinations to meet these three criteria. Perhaps it is more possible when dealing with straightforward *objective* topics (such as basic arithmetic) where there is a correct answer. It is certainly very hard to achieve when dealing with topics where *subjective* answers are called for. Many general management areas call for subjective responses that blend theory with practical experience.

A manager in a large office with responsibility for twenty staff reporting through three supervisors will often have to make a judgement about the quality of the work of a team, the quality of an individual's contribution to the overall success of the team, and a judgement about the composition of each team. Whilst some objective facts are available (volume of work produced, for example) the most important judgement calls are about inter-personal skills and team effectiveness. These inter-personal skill judgements are subjective and based very much upon judgement tempered by experience.

Examinations also have serious defects in mental and physical terms. Coming as they do at stated times and often only offered once a year, they provide a **big bang** end to a course of study. If a student is unwell, or off colour on the day — too bad.

Mentally, examinations are bad news for most people. Because they are so important and because so much hangs upon them, they assume a mystique all their own. People panic in exams! Good students do less well (sometimes fail) through nerves, fear or panic.

Students also fail through physical causes. Anyone who is unwell or off colour on the day of the exam is at a disadvantage. It is also possible to miss an exam completely and be set back six or twelve months until it is offered again.

There is little need to go on, the case is made:

(a) for most people examinations are bad news;

(b) mental and physical pressures hinder accurate judgement (which is what exams are supposed to be for);

(c) reliability, validity and comparability are extremely hard to ensure, especially in subjects where evaluation and judgement are called for.

It is not surprising that there has been a determined move away from examinations, where this is possible. In some areas it isn't possible. An independent body such as a professional institute with a need to examine in a wide range of centres (probably across the world) simply has no other method available. Certainly not one that is anywhere near as fair as the examination system that has developed over many years.

Many professional bodies have transformed their examinations, however. From being simply opportunities to regurgitate facts crammed in the night before, many exams now require candidates to put knowledge and skills to use in the exam room. Thus we are seeing more exams where the "open book" rule applies.

An open book exam is one where candidates are allowed to take material with them into the exam room. The paper can then be structured very differently from a traditional "write five essays" type. Candidates can be tested on their ability to deal with problems set within situations (case studies). Their skill as well as their knowledge can be tested.

The major problem with exams — *big bang* — cannot be overcome. For students *big bang* time is bad news. There has to be a better way. **Continuous assessment** is a better way.

Under continuous assessment, each student's progress is measured, and reported back to him or her. The reporting back is very important. It allows students to see how their work is being judged, where they are strong and where more work is needed. It makes evaluation part of the learning process. It minimises the judgmental element. It allows the student an opportunity to discuss work with tutors, and usually offers the opportunity for re-submission of work that is below standard.

Continuous assessment allows the tutors to stretch the students in ways that are not possible under traditional "tutor centred" teaching. With well thought through assignments a wide range of knowledge and skills can be built up. A course based upon continuous assessment will use written assignments (reports rather than essays), research based projects, oral presentations and demonstrations. The range will be limited only by the objectives of the course, the industry from which the students come and the imagination of the tutor(s). Frequently an assignment will require a combination of various types of work from the student. Continuous assessment, at its best, mirrors the work for which the students are being trained. Yet it has a purpose far wider than training. It is of genuine educational value, with a purpose far wider than a simple training exercise.

Integrity is the key word in continuous assessment. It depends upon the professional integrity of the tutor(s) and of the external moderators.

Students recruited with integrity should not fail a continuously assessed course. Some do, of course, but not many. The high pass rate is largely because the tutors are encouraged to select very carefully. Tutors are under great pressure to succeed and their success is judged through their students. Thus if a student is not doing as well as expected it is the tutor who has to explain why to a moderating panel.

Construction of a course based upon continuous assessment

1. A lead tutor in a centre will be designated. The title may be Course Co-ordinator, Course Tutor, or Course Director.

2. A team of tutors will construct the skeleton of the course, using the guidelines provided by the "body" that they want to validate the course. (A validating body is an independent board or council, such as the National Examinations Board for Supervisory Management — NEBSM.)

3. Approaches will be made to the validating body at this stage to ensure that what is being planned is likely to meet their criteria, and will gain their validation. (Without validation a course only carries the certificate of the centre. With validation, the students are awarded the certificate or diploma of the outside body. Thus the problem of comparability is taken into account.)

4. It may be that a moderator will be attached to the course at this stage. Perhaps this will happen later, but happen it will. A moderator is appointed by the validating body to ensure that the standards of the body are maintained. He or she will have full access to all course records, will visit the course often, get to know the students and the tutors, will moderate all work set by the tutors and will authorise the issue of certificates and/or diplomas. He or she will be from outside the centre and will have a record of running courses that fully meet the body's standards.

5. The course will be constructed in considerable detail. Educational jargon changes constantly and different bodies have their individual terminology, so it is necessary to understand exactly what each term means. The course will be set out in terms of *learning achievement*, not in terms of academic judgement. You will know exactly what you have to show you understand and what skills you have to show that you possess.

Continuous Assessment Explained

6. When the course is ready, and fully documented, it will usually be submitted to an internal board within the centre. At this board the course team will be questioned very closely about the detail of the course and will have to justify its credibility. Only after this has been done, and perhaps after a re-submission, will formal permission to offer the course be applied for.

7. The validating body will carry out its own review of the course proposal and decide whether it is willing to validate it. If so, for how long and under what conditions. Validation is by no means automatic!

8. Once validated, the course can be offered by the centre. Students can be recruited. Teaching can begin.

9. A system of monitoring will have been included in the proposal and it is the course tutor's task to ensure that it is followed. He or she has the moderator to answer to, and moderation is usually friendly but close.

10. Providing the course team delivers what it proposed there is every expectation that *every student will pass.* If students are not doing well enough, this will be picked up early and the course tutor will have some questions to answer. This is taken very seriously indeed, for it is recognised that continuous assessment has the potential for abuse. Integrity is essential, and integrity is best ensured when it is monitored!

11. At the end of the course a full review will be held and the monitor will report back to the validating body. If all is well the course will continue. If not, modifications will be required.

12. In due time successful centres will achieve a reputation and be granted a special status. From then on it will be easier to achieve validation. In these cases the validating body usually requires a specific tutor to be nominated. This tutor will have a direct responsibility to the validating body for all courses running and proposed.

A course running under continuous assessment can contain examinations. Many do. But these exams are not the big bang exams that have been typical of education throughout the decades.

Exams are only one part of a continuous assessment plan of evaluation.

Courses vary considerably in their format and in their methods of assessment. Remember that the format is constructed with the needs of the students in mind, thus the objective of evaluation is primarily to help the students learn. Not to judge or to be critical or destructive.

The exam(s) will occupy a known percentage of the overall evaluation. A typical "weighting" for evaluation may be:

Course work	50% of total marks
Project	25% of total marks
Examinations	25% of total marks.

Each student will have to secure a pass mark in each course work, in the project and in the exams — but there is often a provision to allow an overall average to be applied. (Students must "obtain an overall average mark of 50%, with a minimum of 40% in any one element of the course".)

This flexibility allows individuals scope to have an off day. And to have better and worse subjects. A student doing well throughout the year, achieving marks in the mid-sixties, ought to do well in the exams. If he or she doesn't shine, but pulls in 40%, then the overall pass is achieved.

Better for everybody is the fact that students have constant feedback on achievement throughout the year. Each has many detailed opportunities to review work that is below standard and to consolidate areas of particular strength.

Remember that any examination is set and marked by the course tutors under moderation. This removes the fear of having to sit a paper set by a totally unknown person who is very distant from the student. The tutor has control over what is asked and how to best frame the questions to achieve a controlled evaluation of the learning achieved by the students on a particular course, at a particular time.

Ambiguity can sometimes creep into an examination paper. Sometimes it is not picked up despite detailed scrutiny — until a student detects it. With an externally set exam, the student is on his or her own. With continuous assessment it is possible, and proper, to ask for a tutor's guidance in the exam room. Integrity again is vital. A tutor will help with a genuine ambiguity and will ensure that every student has the point explained. A tutor will not help with a misunderstanding or a misreading that is the student's fault. The object is specifically *not* to help students cheat, nor to allow it. Rather, it is to ensure that the students are not misled by a genuine error that has got through the system.

Finally, in this general introduction, note that an appeals procedure will be set down in the course documentation. Should there be any serious question of discrepancy in marking standard, for example, the matter can be raised through easily accessed channels. We shall look at this in Chapter 9. For the moment let us establish that the appeals procedure is for genuine and serious problems. In most cases a problem is simply a misunderstanding between student and tutor and can be sorted out on a one to one basis, perhaps with the intervention of the course tutor.

It is very important to understand from the very first day exactly what form of evaluation applies to your course. All of your planning for success comes from a thorough grasp of the "rules" under which you are to work. A course is very similar to a game, and you wouldn't play very well without finding out what you were to play — hockey, lacrosse or tennis. Even in tennis you would need to know if you were playing doubles or singles!

SUMMARY

- Measurement of success is necessary.

- Continuous assessment provides individual feedback throughout a course.

- The performance across the whole course will be the basis for evaluation.

- Students must find out *exactly* what are the evaluation criteria.

- Integrity is the key to success in continuous assessment.

- Students recruited with integrity should pass.

EVERY STUDENT SHOULD PASS.

Chapter 8
Continuous Assessment — The Personalities

Who are the personalities that have an impact upon you whilst on your course? It is important that you should know. And that you should understand what motivates them; what is most likely to have them respond favourably to you and your needs.

These are the most likely people to have an influence upon your success — but you may want to add others from your own experience. Let's call this your *influencers list*.

Your employer

Your spouse, and/or parent(s)

Your friends

Your workmates

Your course tutor

Your project tutor

Individual tutors

The assessor

The moderator

The external adviser(s)

The examiners.

When asked about the importance of any of these, most students come up blank. Many have not even considered the impact that any one of them can have on success or failure, or on enjoying or detesting. But it is important to have them on your side, or at least neutral. We shall come back to these people in a little while. First we have to establish an essential principle.

Essential principle — management course students are NOT school children!

Do you agree? You are not a school child? Good. Then why behave like one? Most students approach a course, in a college particularly, as though they were going to school. Unfortunately the habits learned in schools in the United Kingdom over recent years are not helpful to managers on a management course.

You have to shake off school experiences (good as well as bad) and learn afresh. What do you have to learn? To manage your own learning with the help of the tutors.

Management tutors will not exert discipline to force you to learn. They expect you to be self-motivated. Timekeeping is your job. There are no bells ringing to mark the end of periods. You have to get yourself back from coffee breaks on time. The class will start without you, so you will quickly learn — but it can be a painful experience and it need not be.

Never refer to assignments as "homework". That term carries very bad vibes for most people. If you don't want to do the assignment, then don't. But don't expect a tutor to bully you for it and don't expect to pass the course!

Some students even revert to disruptive classroom tactics. Great fun! But why do it? And why should you tolerate it? If you are unfortunate enough to find an overgrown school kid in your class then take steps yourself to help him or her to shape up or ship out. Management courses are made up of teams. Teams of tutors and students with several aims:

Continuous Assessment — The Personalities

(a) to help everyone benefit from the course from day one;

(b) to secure a pass for everyone on the course, if possible;

(c) to help everyone enjoy their time on the course.

It is up to every member of the team to pull together and in the same direction.

You must do your share to ensure that the course is not a waste of time and that you benefit from it positively. You will know when you notice, probably with some degree of surprise, that you are doing things differently at work and in your social life. The course, if it is working *for* you, will work *on* you. You will change. *Learning is demonstrated through a change of behaviour* — remember? Take note of your behaviour from time to time; your friends and colleagues will notice changes, so it is good to check with them. Personal benefit is the real value; the bonus is the qualification.

Your influencers list will be useful now. Let us couple it with a technique of problem analysis. Your problem is that you do not know enough about those on your list. You would like to know more — you need to know more; then you will be able to achieve maximum benefit from the course and give a fair return to those who are investing in you.

People are investing in you. Your employer is obviously doing so, by releasing you, by paying fees and so on. Your spouse and/or parents are sacrificing some of the time that otherwise they could be spending with you; your better tutors are working with you above and beyond the level to which they are contracted. For each there has to be a return. If you can discover what it is you can do something about ensuring that you deliver. Then the course is not about your totally selfish gaining of enjoyment, training, qualification.

Here is an analytical tool that you should use right now. You will need to use it for every person on your influencers list, but your time will be well spent. You will find that you will be able to group several of your influencers — but be careful to only do this if you are certain the grouping is valid. Think through very carefully to see if the superficial resemblance is totally genuine.

The first thing you need is an objective. Why are you doing the analysis? What will come from it? Your objective is *that you gain insight into the motivations and value judgements of others in order that you may be better equipped to succeed on your course.*

Take a sheet of A4, turn it sideways and put the four headings across:

STRENGTHS	WEAKNESSES	MOTIVATIONS	INCENTIVES

Then produce an itemised list under each heading. (Use a mind map for the initial analysis.) You will need to carry out a separate analysis for each person on your influencers list. Take about an hour. You should then have a series of basic lists that will form the framework onto which you will build an understanding of each person and the perceptual base from which they are working. Once you know where a person is coming from, what their value judgement system is based upon, what they expect in return for their personal investment, you are in a strong position to ensure that you meet their expectations and deliver in the terms most of value to each individual.

The present tendency is to involve employers as important members of the course team. The title "external adviser" is used by BTEC. Whatever they are called, employers are on the team to ensure that the course turns out students who are credible employees in the current marketplace. Some courses use their external advisers very actively. They will meet the students and teach on the residential period; others use them as advisers, with little or no direct access to the students.

You will have your own views on the people who have a direct impact upon you but, as an example, let us examine the profile of a typical assessor. We are taking this example because it is the one you will have least knowledge about, and the assessor is a person about whom you may feel some concern. (The title assessor is used by NEBSM and moderator is used by BTEC. Their duties are very similar and their impact on the course from the students' viewpoint is identical. We shall use the title assessor, for simplicity, in this section of the book.)

WHO IS A TYPICAL ASSESSOR?

Some students are frightened by the assessor. Or perhaps they are frightened by the *concept* of the assessor. Do they want to believe in the infallibility of assessors; do they gain a sense of security in that way? If so, it is all part of the myths surrounding the academic world. Myths that we have created. Myths that you must take very seriously — examine, test and master. You have to accept that assessors are *people,* important, yes, but *people.* Humans.

Once we can accept that assessors are people — that they have human strengths and weaknesses — then we can get on with the business of playing to their strengths and benefiting from their weaknesses. Throughout the rest of life we are very interested in other peoples' strengths and weaknesses (it is necessary to survival). We have examined our own earlier, so we must examine the assessor's. So, who are assessors?

Probable assessor

Age:

Between 35 and 75, because sufficient experience, status and the time to be an assessor is unlikely to be achieved before 35, and assessment is a task that can be carried on with great credibility after normal retirement age.

Sex:

Either, although they are still predominantly male in the United Kingdom. But only because women have yet to make it to the top in sufficient numbers across the whole of United Kingdom management.

Background:

Very high probability of an academic background. Your assessor is likely to be a tutor working with students day by day. Certainly he or she will have practical experience teaching, probably as a course tutor to the course you are taking, but in a different centre.

He or she could be the head of business in a college, run a correspondence course, be a consultant. He or she is unlikely to be in a nine to five job in industry.

He or she is likely to be an author of textbooks or articles for professional journals.

Qualifications:

High probability of a Masters' Degree as well as a first degree. Experience in teaching the subject. Evidence of a positive academic contribution such as authorship or success in coaching students through exams.

Possibly experience in using his or her subject in "real life".

Recruitment:

Various sources but certainly with the supporting recommendation(s) of respected colleagues.

Are you asking, *so what?* What value is this analysis to you?

Seriously, how can this chapter help *you?* Can you see a way?

Continuous Assessment — The Personalities

Let us consider the assessors' strengths and weaknesses.

Also consider what will motivate an assessor, and what incentives he or she is likely to respond to.

Strengths:

Academic knowledge and ability.

Experience of course teaching, probably course tutoring.

Trusted member of the validating body.

Approves the course programme, enforces the rules.

Personal self-confidence, reinforced by the recognition and status of the post.

Professional integrity.

Meets the students, gets to know something of them personally.

Weaknesses:

Limited time actually in contact with the course.

Reliant, to some degree, on the integrity of the course tutor.

Constrained by the system — it is expected that students will pass.

Works within the syllabus and the rules.

Responds to his or her unconscious mind — the sixth sense.

Motivations:

Vocation — Sense of fitness for a career or occupation.

Integrity — An assessor's integrity is valued highly.

Pride — An appointment as an assessor is a mark of achievement; within the academic world especially.

Status — An assessor's post gives status and *recognition* from one's colleagues.

Power — An assessor is in possession of secret information and holds the responsibility of exercising judgement over the candidates' work.

Incentives:

Primary — Contribution(s) to the body of academic knowledge.

— Satisfaction from student success. (Really!)

— Pleasure from the successful and smooth running of a course for which he or she is responsible.

Secondary — Qualifications (eg Fellowship of an Institute).

— Extension of personal cv. Opportunity for advancement.

— *Not* money as an assessor — assessors are paid an honorarium, and they could all earn much more doing something else.

— Pleasure at meeting the course team on the residential weekend.

Do you agree that your assessor is likely to be a very well educated person. A man, most probably, from at least one generation ahead of most candidates.

His sense of values will, therefore, have been formed within a different society to the one now existing. (He cannot be expected to fully share *your* world, not to be totally in command of current jargon.)

He will be fully in touch with new developments, he will read far more widely than most students. He will be in touch with the contemporary marketplace. He will be able to cross reference your course against others that he is assessing in your centre, in other centres, and against those being assessed by his colleagues.

The assessor is motivated differently from the "average man". We all have special skills — those of the assessor are very special. It is not an easy thing to go into a centre where fellow academics are working at producing a course and be the one who finds fault with it. Academics have very short fuses as a rule, and do not take kindly to their work being judged. Therefore, a considerable degree of tact is required if an assessor is to be effective. Tact combined with efficiency and effectiveness is a rare commodity. Don't underestimate your assessor.

Your assessor will have been carefully chosen and will be subject to on-going review. Assessor appointments are not for life. They are on fixed terms but can be extended if both parties (the validating body and the assessor) agree. The centre for which the assessor is responsible has a say too. Extension is dependent on results, as in the rest of life.

Moderation is taken very seriously by validating bodies. BTEC, for example, produces a moderators handbook which sets out the criteria that must be met and gives both general and specific guidance. Assessors must visit their centre at regular intervals and a detailed report has to be compiled (see Appendix B). This report is copied to the course tutor, via his or her principal. It therefore has high impact and gives the assessor a very strong influence (if not actual power) over the quality of the course.

How do you get the assessor to notice you, especially?

There are two basic principles: *Impress* and *simplify*.

1. *Impress*— You and your work have to stand out as *good*. Note: the assessor will make a judgement about you *as a person*, as well as about the quality of your work. Be

yourself — don't try to impress (don't show off, or be pushy). Do be careful to dress and behave in a manner appropriate to a manager in your business.

2. *Simplify—* Make sure that you think through any questions so that they come out in a structure that he or she will understand. Answer questions directly. If you don't know, say so. If appropriate, go on to say how you will find out, or when you expect the topic to be covered (eg "We haven't come to that topic yet; it comes up just after Christmas.")

You will meet your assessor, usually early in a course, also at the residential weekend and at any oral examination. Take the trouble to make yourself known; establish for yourself what kind of person he or she is. Find out what his or her expectations of you are. (You may not agree with them, but you must know what they are.)

Similarly you must be aware of the standards and expectation of everybody on your influencers list. Some tutors are punctual and hold rigidly to set deadlines; some are relaxed; perhaps one is casual. Your response should be tailored so far as possible to the needs of the tutors. You know this unconsciously, of course; one makes these adjustments in behaviour all the time. The difference suggested here is that you make a deliberate effort to analyse what adjustments you need to make to ensure the best possible response from each individual influencer. Here are two examples:

1. *A cynical student on a course recently was about to hand in an assignment. A colleague picked it up and read it over coffee. "Hey, you can't submit this, it's not accurate — it's behind the times!" "So is the tutor" was the reply.*

2. *A whole class of students clubbed together to buy copies of an economics text written by their tutor (it wasn't the set book). Not bad thinking — except that (a) the tutor never set or marked any assignments or exams and (b) he was due to retire in six weeks.*

When working on a course that is personally assessed you must take advantage of the opportunities that are built in to the system. You know who will be marking your work. You know who you will meet on an oral interview. You have the opportunity to build up a reputation over a period of time. Thus you must work *with* your tutors and *with* your assessor. They know what they want. You have every opportunity to discover what it is, and present it to them.

The KISS principle is invaluable:

Keep It Short and Simple.

Far too many students complicate matters for themselves. Just go with the flow, do exactly what is asked in assignments and examinations, and you'll pass with flying colours.

The same principles apply when dealing with people exterior to your course. Parents and/or spouses are entitled to share something of your course with you; they are helping you to take the course if only by not pressuring you out of work on assignments. What you share, in how much detail, is a matter that you must discover.

Employers are entitled to know what is going on in the time when you are away from work and they are paying the bills. Would you like it if an employee was away every Thursday for a year and never reported back on what he or she was doing? It doesn't have to be much of a contact either. A simple word or two about the course and your progress is often enough.

There is a major opportunity that you shouldn't miss. That is the chance to ask your boss for help on an assignment. You will find that you will need help sometimes, so include your boss on the list of those you can approach. He or she will be flattered and impressed if the work is harder than he or she expected you to be coping with. When you do ask for help, remember to go back after the assignment is returned and say thanks.

SUMMARY

➤ Make an influencers list.

➤ Analyse the relationships between the course, yourself and each member of the list.

➤ Behave as a self-motivated adult; do not drop back into school habits.

➤ Self-monitor to measure how your behaviour is changing.

➤ Involve your family; don't shut them out.

➤ Involve your employer. Report back regularly.

➤ Impress and simplify.

➤ KISS — Keep It Short and Simple.

ASSESSORS AND TUTORS WANT YOU TO PASS.

Chapter 9
Continuous Assessment —
Its Importance to Students

Continuous assessment is a boon and a blessing for students on a general management course, in comparison to the alternative. The alternative is an end-of-session *big bang* examination which results in a pass or a fail. The motivation for big bang exams doesn't hit students until a few weeks before, and in many cases topics covered early in the course may as well never have been bothered with. It all has to be "re-learned" — crammed into the short-term memory in the weeks or days before the examinations.

Not only is this traumatic for the students, it is extremely wasteful in terms of learning, and therefore of improved behaviour in jobs and social life. It is better by far for understanding to come through use, and for the use to be not theoretical in class, but a blend of theory and practical experience.

Continuous assessment, especially when coupled with a course spread between a centre and work, is a most effective means to achieve real learning, useful learning.

It is not normal for students to appreciate this at first! Courses based upon continuous assessment are a continuing source of pain to some of them. Always there is a deadline (or two, or three) coming up. Always there is appraisal, judgement, criticism, pressure. But these are the negative attitudes of students who are working against the system and against themselves.

The positive virtues of appraisal and judgement are in the opportunities for praise and in the guidance that can be given whilst a subject is still being learned; in the freedom to turn to tutors for help before committing oneself to an assignment; in the personal tutorials that can follow an assignment; in the fallback opportunity to resubmit if the need arises.

Some students come to a course expecting a form of brain transplant. They expect that tutors, by some form of magic incantation, will implant the necessary knowledge and skills. They believe that any work from a student is a bonus for the tutor. Tutors meet this attitude all the time and it can be very wearing. The sad truth is, of course, that learning is an individual matter than cannot be forced from the outside. Incentives can be offered but the motivation to learn must come from within.

There is no doubt that getting the brain started can be painful. It acts like an old rusty machine full of cogs and wheels and levers that have not moved in ages, but which are still connected properly together. The effort to get that machinery into motion is considerable: you have to decide if it is worth it.

If you were dying of thirst in a desert and came on an old water pump that had seized up you would exert every effort to get it working; if you thirst after knowledge and skills you will struggle with your inbuilt laziness.

We are all born lazy. Our natural inclination is to take the easiest route. There is nothing wrong in this — in fact, the busiest people often claim to be the laziest. They work to establish a simple routine to rid themselves of the chore of doing work the hard way. Their chosen hard work is mental, not physical.

The benefit of well planned continuous assessment is that it encourages you to pick up speed gradually. You won't be over-extended (but you may feel that you are). When students look back after completing a course they are astonished how much work they are now capable of: far more than they had dreamed of when they started the course. It will be the same for you, but you must stick to it in the early days.

A mature student (of 40) went to a teachers' training college 24 years after leaving school. The culture shock was tremendous and the workload seemed impossible. The solution, in this case, was to concentrate simply on what could be done, to shut out tomorrow and next week, to survive. After two weeks it was possible to open up a little and by the fifth week he was beginning to enjoy the experience. He passed the course with flying colours, was offered a job in a further education college and has made a career out of teaching. But in the middle of the second week the depression was so intense that he seriously considered if he was capable of handling the material.

The student described is the author of this book, so the accuracy of the anecdote is guaranteed. The trauma of those first two weeks is still remembered but the overwhelming benefits of forcing the mind to become active again far outweigh the short term effort.

There is an old wives' tale that aged people find it harder to learn. Perhaps they do, but it is nothing to do with their physical abilities. The brain is just as capable in a fit person at 60 as at 16. Too often, however, the 60 year old has allowed the brain to settle into a comfortable series of routines. It is breaking out of these routines that causes the pain; the pain causes the person to shut down, when shut down a brain cannot learn.

True learning can be painful. One is asking the brain to accept new material or to adjust previously held beliefs. Worse, sometimes one is asked to justify a position. That can be a very hard experience. In the social world we give out an opinion, and do not have to analyse, let alone explain, why we hold that opinion. On a course one is expected to form an opinion and to be able to say, very clearly, why; also to defend the opinion against argument. This is hard, but necessary. Otherwise we would exist in a world that was managed by people taking decisions based on little more than hunch or guesswork. (The cynics among you will now be saying "But we are".)

Of course there are good managers and bad ones. But the good far outweigh the bad, and the good take the time to think through a problem. As you will discover from your studies the best management is about taking decisions and giving support to staff. A good manager will have a systematic ability to analyse a situation, create alternative solutions, evaluate each and to choose one. This happens naturally to only a very few. And even these few find that the challenge of the right course is of benefit in improving their abilities.

Continuous assessment allows each and every student to have prompt feedback on his or her progress. If a standard is not being reached there is opportunity for personal tuition and for an assignment to be resubmitted.

This is far better than working for a year towards an external examination and then passing (or not) without any notion as to why or how. Passing in this case is not so bad, but failing, without indication of the weakness can be very damaging to the motivation. Especially when a friend who normally does worse than you gets a pass! (Probably it was a silly mistake, made in the heat of the exam room, that let you down but you don't know.)

It is quite usual for students to take away a false impression from an examination. To think they have done badly and be surprised when their pass comes through. Or to feel badly let down by a fail. Think about it and you will understand why.

The candidate is exposed to the exam paper for a maximum of three hours. In that time it is necessary to digest the paper as a whole, read and understand the questions, select the ones to answer, plan answers, write answers, check through, and get name and/or candidate number on to every piece of exam stationery. Whatever a tutor says, however hard a student tries, there will inevitably be some degree of stress, and under stress we do things that are abnormal.

Our sense of perception lets some of us down and we carry away a false impression of the paper and of our achievement.

Sometimes, with continuous assessment, it is possible to obtain help even after an examination. A student taking a management course was very surprised to find his exam mark down to 55% when his assignments had all been marked at over 90%. (So was his tutor!)

The tutor was able to access the examination script and, on this rare occasion, secured permission to show it to the student. It was nothing like the student remembered. He was distressed by the scrappy work he had submitted when under pressure. He learnt a valuable lesson; the course as a whole benefited (since he stopped complaining about how his paper had been unfairly marked), and the importance of continuous assessment as a fairer way to evaluate learning was reinforced.

MANAGING TIME

To succeed on a course it is essential to manage your time. With continuous assessment a plan will exist showing when each assignment is due to be issued and returned. This plan will provide for a scheduled workload and will assume that you are allocating sufficient time when away from college for the work to be completed.

There are two points to remember:

1. The schedule will not work as planned. Don't ever expect it to. Lots of things will happen — a tutor will go sick; a photocopier will break down; bad weather will close the centre for a week.

2. Your use of time must be able to accommodate the shifts in the schedule.

There is no need, for example, to wait until an assignment is issued. If you don't know what topic it will cover, you can ask. Then you can start to prepare yourself to answer it. Work through your notes on the topic, check it out in the texts. It won't be time wasted. When you get the assignment do be sure to read it extremely carefully. Be sure you answer what is asked for, it may not be what you have prepared for.

A silly, but tragic example, is of the student who would have been top in her year. She came second because when asked for an assignment on marketing research she submitted one on marketing. It is so very easy to do and if you do it you will have only yourself to blame.

Ask your course tutor how much time you should allow outside class. Be prepared for the answer "at least as much as you spend in the classroom".

You must set your diary up with clear space for your course work, and do ensure that deadline dates for assignments are entered very clearly.

When planning time for your project (assuming you have one to do) consider how much time you need, add on 50% and then double it. Projects are incredibly time consuming, especially if they are badly planned, as we shall see in Chapter 12.

You may be unlucky enough to have a tutor who is not covering an area as you would wish. For some reason you are not learning. You must not waste time (and going to the lesson is a waste of time). What to do?

First diagnose your problem.

1. What is the problem? Is it you?

    Are you reading ahead, are you truly working? Are you expecting the material to magically transfer itself from tutor to you?

    There is an old joke about the transfer of notes from the tutor's file to the student's — without going through the brains of either.

2. Are others finding the same problem with the tutor? How do you

know? Are they telling you, or are you asking them? Are you individually or as a group whining about the problem, but not taking any action?

Your first action **must** *be to speak with the tutor concerned. Have a quiet word. Don't complain, just have a word. Your objective is to learn, not to instigate a confrontation!*

3. Is it the tutor, or is it the topic?

    Some topics are very hard to teach, and some are very hard to learn — for general management students. Statistics and law are high on the list of hate subjects. Even the very best tutors have difficulty in communicating what others regard as dry subjects, but the problem is usually with the student, not the tutor.

    Unfortunately it is not uncommon to find that students who complain about a law tutor, for example, haven't even bought the set text book, let alone tried to read it!

4. It is the tutor; others feel the same. A quiet word doesn't help.

    The approach now must be to the course tutor. You will have a student who represents the course on the course board. It is best to get the rep to approach the course tutor, again quietly; but be prepared to raise the issue formally at the course board if you have to.

    Remember: *You are raising an issue that will affect the career of the tutor, so be very sure that you are justified in raising an official complaint, and that there is no alternative.*

Every course will have a defined appeals procedure which will be open to you. Through it you will be able to appeal against decisions and raise complaints about any aspect of the course. Be certain that you have a genuine complaint *before* you start formal proceedings, and be certain that you are prepared to go *all the way* if necessary. Centres take formal complaints very seriously and the procedures are structured to give a student the right to reach the very top of the organisation if the complaint is not resolved at a lower level. The best advice is not to get involved in a formal procedure unless there is absolutely no alternative.

Whatever the outcome, there will still be a need for you to pass in the topic. Even if you secure a change of tutor (quite unlikely given the difficulty of recruiting specialist staff) you face the short term problem of getting a high enough mark and the long term problem of understanding the topic so that you can utilise it at work.

You are an adult, taking a management course. Therefore you manage your time. If you will be better out of the class, in the library doing private study, then go to the library. (But do have the courtesy to say, quietly, to the tutor that is what you are doing. And do work in the library, don't slip off to the cafe for an extended coffee break.)

Any of these actions calls for courage on your part. But courage you have to have as a manager. You have to analyse the problem, decide on alternative courses of action, evaluate their cost benefit and decide on a course of action. Then remember to evaluate the result. Was it worthwhile? Would you do it again? Differently or the same?

SUMMARY

➤ Continuous assessment provides monitoring, feedback and help — but doesn't remove the need for students to work.

➤ Nobody says that learning is easy.

➤ Don't expect too much, too soon.

➤ Manage your time.

➤ Take each assignment as it comes, don't try to plan too far forward.

➤ Hit your deadlines.

➤ Trust your tutors, but don't expect them to be perfect.

➤ Take charge of your own learning.

LEARN IN THE WAY THAT IS BEST FOR YOU.

Section Three

Course Work

Chapter 10
Success in Assessment

Success in assessment comes from several key factors:

1. Knowing exactly what the assessment scheme for the course is, overall.
2. Understanding exactly what is required in each part of the assessment scheme.
3. Understanding exactly what is required in each assignment.
4. Meeting the exact requirements.

This may seem obvious, but students continuously do badly in assignments through not understanding what is required. Or through understanding the requirement, but then not delivering it!

There is a carefully structured system, as explained in Chapter 7, which will be followed to specify the assessment procedure for your course. The tutors are bound by it. As a student you can only benefit from gaining a detailed understanding of it. It is *not* secret. It is *not* being awkward to ask for it. Please do not be bashful. If your course tutor doesn't issue the full details very early in your course — **ask for them**.

Having got the assessment system, work at understanding it. There may well be some educational jargon that you haven't met before. Ask your tutor to explain anything you don't understand. *Do not* ask fellow students — they may believe they understand, but how will you know if they do? Or if they don't?

WHY ASSESS?

Assessment has two main purposes:

1. To measure the level of achievement attained by each student in respect of a specific course objective.
2. To determine, by the end of the course, whether individual students have passed or failed.

Measurement = feedback

On a course which operates under continuous assessment you get feedback as you progress from week to week. Success is not determined by a big bang examination set at the end of the course (perhaps eight or nine months since a topic was covered in class). Regular feedback tells you exactly how well you are doing. It also helps the tutors to make judgements about their teaching plans and introduce changes if necessary.

As the course progresses, the work you are set will become progressively tougher; the early work sets a foundation for the later material. So please do not worry if you see work from the third term of your course. You may think that it is beyond you. It probably is — now! It is beyond all students at your stage of the course! But it won't be beyond you when it is issued after two terms' experience.

Your course will be set up using sub-objectives to develop your learning (see diagram opposite).

PASS OR FAIL

There is no need even to consider failure. Why should you fail? Hand

Success in Assessment

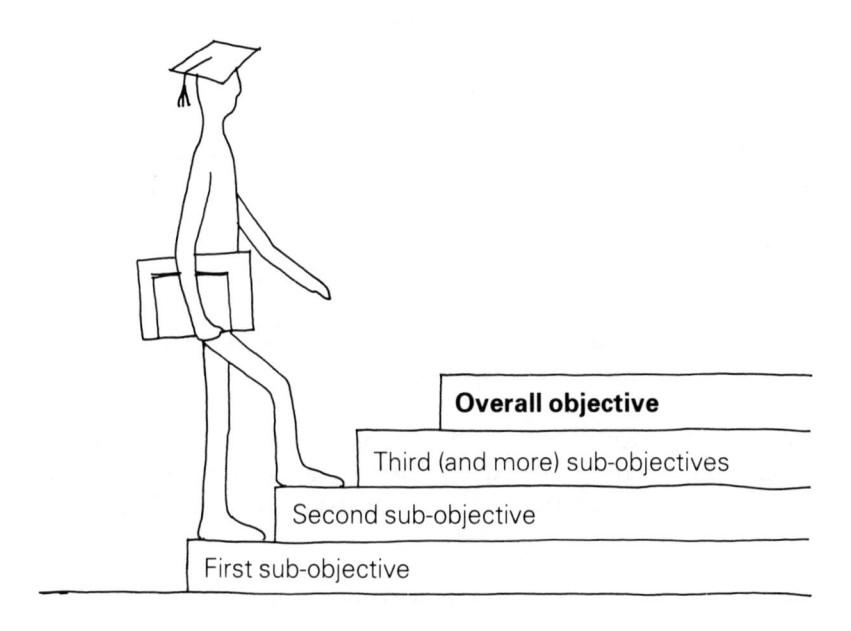

| Overall objective |
| Third (and more) sub-objectives |
| Second sub-objective |
| First sub-objective |

Your course will be set up using sub-objectives to develop your learning

your work in on time *and* take notice of the feedback that you receive. Then you will know your areas of strength and weakness. You will know how your marks are building up. You will know in which areas you have to work harder — or ask for tutorial help. You will be working from knowledge, not from hope. Most of the fear (which is of failure) is removed.

The *vast majority* of students working under continuous assessment pass their courses. They are meant to. Recruited with integrity, taught with consideration, and protected by the assessment framework, it is rare for a student to fail. Some leave the course because the workload is too much for them (or is their motivation too low?). But for those who work through to the end it is rare for anything other than a pass or distinction to be awarded.

You must carry your share of the learning load — a tutor cannot do your learning for you. In fact all instruction in imperfect. There is no way that a tutor can do a perfect job of *teaching* for every student. *Instruction* is a joint effort. It involves you in learning. (Teaching can be done to an empty room! It is a one-way process.)

It follows that if you know how to learn and you know what you are supposed to learn, you will have a greater likelihood of success.

An old teacher, worried, says to a younger colleague: "But if I tell them what to study for, won't they all get it right?"

The young tutor replies: "Of course! And if they don't it will be for you to go over the material again until they do..."

With continuous assessment it is your *learning* that is being measured, in terms of knowledge, skill and attitude. As you develop, so your learning opportunities will be widened and your abilities will increase to meet the challenge.

One of the major strengths of continuous assessment is its ability to allow you to work from your strengths and repair your weaknesses. You will be able to learn from other students, as well as from tutors and books. You will find that you will be able to coach others in some topics but need help from others who are strong in topics where you are weaker. (What a valuable lesson for a manager under training!)

ASSESSMENT METHODS

Assessment is always related to the aims and objectives of the course. At present there is an almost equal split between different management courses regarding the form of the actual assessment, and its recording. Some use the well known method of awarding marks, others assign grades. (As has been explained in Chapter 7 there is in reality very little for you to bother about, whichever method is used on your course.)

In both cases, at the end of the course you will achieve one of five results: you will pass with distinction, pass with merit, pass, be referred, fail. If you are referred it may mean an "invitation" to retake a single subject examination, or you may be "invited" to retake the whole course. Referral is only offered to those who, in the opinion of the course board, have every opportunity of securing a pass. Usually the cause of the referral will be well known, a student may have been away for six weeks and missed a vital component of the course, or a student with an excellent record may submit an awful examination paper. (Exam nerves hit some people harder than others.)

On the CMS you can now only pass, be referred, or fail.

Remember that the intention is for you to pass; that the tutorial team are focussed upon you passing; that tutors gain respect by running good courses that pass people. There is no kudos to be gained by a tutor from failing a student. In fact, to fail a student involves the tutor in considerably more work than giving a pass! *Do not be misled into thinking that everyone passes automatically. Of course they do not. Tutors have integrity and will fight for their right to fail a student if they feel they have to.*

Passes are earned on merit. The *quality* of the pass indicates something about the student, but a simple pass is not given as an automatic right.

ASSESSMENT TYPES

The forms of assessment are limited only by the imagination of the tutor team and the needs of the student group. Those in most common use are:

Written assignment

You are required to write a report, sometimes an essay, upon a given topic, and submit it to time. This, very traditional form of student work is most valuable as an encouragement to students to show understanding of underpinning theory. It is necessary for one to understand *why* as well as *how*. The why (of knowledge) can be tested in a simple written assignment before the how (of skill) is tested in some practical way. Obviously a written assignment also allows a student's skills of written communication to be evaluated. (This is important for a management student who will spend most of his or her working life communicating verbally and often at a distance.)

Practical work

You have the opportunity for "hands on" practice. The easiest illustration comes from computing where it is essential not only to know how a program works but to have worked with it. (It is frustrating for a secretary to have a boss who doesn't know the limitations of the equipment he or she is working with. And especially frustrating to have to work below the capability of the hard and/or software.)

Practical work can be in the centre. It can be in one's own time. It can be carried through at work. It can be with or without direct supervision. The Double U principle underpins its value. To truly know, you have to understand *and* use.

Demonstration

Getting up in front of others to demonstrate one's skills is not easy. But it is a useful way of helping you to gain confidence. It can also be a powerful way to develop mutual support within the group. Your diffidence is natural but no tutor will allow a student to be humiliated, and no student group will allow a member to be subjected to unfair and/or harsh criticism. Nothing binds a group together better than an attack on one of its members.

Project

Many students self-inflict trouble over their projects. They are frightened of the project as a concept; they go ill-prepared into the unknown; they do not allow sufficient time; they do not call upon tutors for help. A project is hard work but it can and should be worthwhile and enjoyable. We shall be looking in detail at projects in Chapter 12.

Group assignment

Most managers work as part of a team for most of their lives. It is necessary to learn to harness the knowledge and skills of a group to maximum benefit. It is also necessary to learn how to be a productive member of a team; to learn how leadership actually shifts as a team's needs change; to learn how to help shape attitude so that a team is most effective. Management theory from textbooks gives a foundation but you have to build your own personal ability as a manager.

There are two important points to remember:

(a) you do not have to like someone to work with him or her;

(b) you can't choose your team mates at work.

It follows that you should mix around and work with everyone else on the course at some time. Take the opportunity to learn; don't settle into a cosy peer group and shut the others out. A group assignment will give you every opportunity to mix. It will be structured so that it is too big for any one person to complete in time and it will call for a range of skills. You will *need* that odd person from the other side of the classroom — he or she will be brilliant at something you barely understand!

Practical activity

Again, this is an opportunity for you to do something that will benefit your learning overall. You may be asked to carry out a research survey, to construct a detailed floor plan of your wing of the centre, to build a tower made from Lego bricks. The objectives for the activity will be clear: whatever direct bearing they have on your immediate learning they will also be of indirect benefit to your developing personal skills as a manager.

Personal development journal

This is sometimes called a "log book". It is a record, that you maintain, of your development as the course progresses. There is often reluctance to bother with the journal but its value becomes apparent as time passes. The PDJ is the subject of Chapter 11.

Written examination

Not every management course has written exams, but where they are included it is to provide a test, under controlled conditions, of your abilities as an individual. They are less often tests of memory, more and more they are becoming "open book". Often they attempt to replicate the real world by allowing you plenty of time to acquire a full understanding of a situation described in a "case study" that is issued ahead of the examination. In the exam room you are faced with questions that a boss at work might ask and reasonably expect you to be able to answer from your knowledge and experience of the organisation you work for.

Some use is being made of multiple choice question papers where you are required to select the best answer from a selection.

Clear guidance will be given by the tutors ahead of the exams as an aid to your revision. You will not be expected to go blindly into an exam with no idea of the range and type of questions that may be asked. Section Four covers examinations in detail.

Oral interview

Talking with a moderator gives many students the collywobbles. This is understandable, but it is important that managers be able to communicate in all circumstances. You have to be able to converse with important people (ie the managing director), and it is important to verify your ability to do so. Chapter 20 takes you through the process.

Employer's report

It is now accepted that the learning process is a partnership between individual students, tutors and employers. Any assessment that is based upon performance in the classroom has a built in bias and is incomplete. Many management students are now sponsored onto courses and employers are taking a positive interest in staff development. It is not surprising, therefore, to find that some courses include an assessment of achievement from the employer as one component of the overall assessment.

Peer group

Who knows the true value of each student better than the others on the course? Tutors come and go throughout the course; more and more of the assessment is becoming group based — how can a tutor know if each member of a group has contributed equally? It can be complicated to devise a method that allows students to allocate marks and it has to be done fairly. It is worthwhile, however, since it discourages individuals who free-load on the work of others. It also introduces a discipline that deals with lazy students without anyone having to complain, or "sneak".

One form of peer group marking is for the tutor to allocate a total mark to the group, say 80%. If there are five in the group, that equals 400 marks. Each member of the group then indicates how the 400 should be split between individuals. A weighted average is taken and this is then discussed, modified if necessary, and agreed by the group. It is a little complicated, but it has benefits in terms of group dynamics as well as in achieving its primary aim of allocating marks more accurately than a tutor would be able to do.

Self-assessment

You mark your own work. Yes, it does sound crazy; but it is surprising how critical self-judgement can be. The usual problem for the tutor in this form of assessment is explaining why the self-mark is too low — and getting it increased by the student!

ASSESSMENT CRITERIA

The criteria used for each assessment will depend upon the objective(s) that are being tested. The overall intention is to pass out students who have reached a level of achievement that merits the award of the CMS, NEBSM, etc. If the requirements of the validating body are known, and they are, it is then possible to work backwards:

(a) What attitudes, knowledge and skills are needed, generally?

(b) What attitude, knowledge and skills are needed, specifically?

(c) Is each criterion specific and unambiguous?

(d) How can each specific criterion be measured?

(e) In which order must they be tested?

(f) How can each best be tested?

Your course will have been put together so that its structure takes you through a series of sub-objectives that interlock across the course as a whole. This may not be apparent to you at a casual glance but if you take some time and examine the course programme you will be comforted to see how well planned it actually is.

Criteria types

These are so wide, and so detailed, that it is better for you to examine those set for your course. There isn't room in this book for full coverage! Some of the more common *general* headings are:

(a) problem solving;

(b) information processing;

(c) numerical ability;

(d) communication, written and oral;

(e) negotiation;

(f) public speaking;

(g) creativity;

(h) time management;

(i) group dynamics.

GOLDEN RULES FOR SUCCESS

(a) Find out before each stage of the course if it is to be assessed.

(b) If it is — by whom, how, when, using what criteria?

(c) Get the assignment or assessment schedule in writing; be sure it is not ambiguous.

(d) Be certain you understand exactly what is required.

(e) Complete the work to time and ensure that it reaches the tutor.

Two horror situations you *must* be prepared for:

1. *The work is completed, to time, and put in the tutor's post tray or on his/her desk. (Or you give it to a friend to deliver.) The tutor claims not to have received it!*

2. *The tutor has the work from you personally — but mislays it! (Or the office cleaner picks up a pile of paper in error and dumps it.)*

You are not to blame but it is *your* problem. No work means no marks. There is no charity in situations like these. The answer is **always to keep a copy of your work**. It is as easy as that.

SUMMARY

➤ Find out the assessment scheme for your course.

➤ Understand each part of it, in detail.

➤ Provide exactly what each assignment requires.

➤ The intention is for you to pass.

➤ Share your knowledge and skills and benefit from the knowledge and skills of others.

ALWAYS KEEP A COPY OF YOUR WORK.

Chapter 11
Personal Development Journal

A management course should stretch you, mentally and physically. If you are not challenged mentally; not having to work hard; not having to exert yourself; you are on the wrong course!

A good course is one which is exhilarating and that you are eager to attend — one that you arrange your holidays around. It will be crammed with incidents, some serious, some amusing, some crucial, some frivolous. But you won't remember most of them.

The process of simply coping with the demands of a home and social life, a full course *and* a job will occupy you fully. There will be no space for you to remember everything that happened. Nor will you notice all that you are learning.

It is important that you notice your learning. You will be growing whilst on the course. Your abilities will increase; you will be smarter/quicker at work; you will begin to use new techniques routinely in normal life; your self-confidence will increase dramatically.

Colleagues will notice, bosses will notice, family will notice, but you may not for a long time. Why? Because the changes are subtle and cumulative. Each tiny increase in your overall level of ability adds a small contribution to the totality that is you. Overall the effect can be staggering. You won't notice because you won't be looking.

A "mature student", who has seen her 50th birthday go past and who finished a year long management course recently, was required to write a summary of her personal learning experience as part of the assessment. This is what she wrote:

"...In personal terms, what I have gained most from the course is an enormous increase in self-confidence. I think I have always known how to present myself in public and to talk to an audience... but it has taken me a long time to feel I can hold my own in such circumstances. This new self-knowledge and self-confidence is already having very positive effects... and has been very important to me..."

It is only when one looks back over an experience, and compares where one is now against where one was, and where one would have been without the course, that the true value can be seen. This is an interesting exercise that you should put yourself through, even if it is not a requirement on your course.

We all have a "role expectation". We know where we fit, most of us are comfortable with the situation that we have been conditioned to accept. But you are in the process of changing your role, of moving to a new position within the established order, of "improving yourself".

Others will begin to expect more of you. Therefore you have to develop the confidence that comes from self-knowledge so that you can maximise the benefits the course is bringing to you.

And, when the course is all over and you have your certificate, it will be good to be able to review the good times, and the bad; to check out how you felt in the early days and compare that to how you feel now; to confirm that the time you have devoted to learning has not been wasted, that the sacrifices made by you *and especially your family* have been worthwhile.

Keeping a diary is an excellent idea. Many people start one each January, but by the second week of the year it lies ignored somewhere, gathering dust. A course diary is also an excellent idea. You will not expect it to be called a diary, of course — the academic world cherishes its own language. Your course diary will be called a personal development journal (PDJ), or a log book.

PURPOSE OF THE PDJ

The PDJ forces you to do something you ought to do for yourself. It requires you to keep a strict record of the course, of your progress, and of your evolving views on management and your own perception of yourself and of your role in management.

Sometimes the PDJ is assessed. On some courses it is assessed at regular intervals, perhaps once a term. On others it is assessed once a year. Some courses award a mark, others use it as a part of an overall appraisal system. Some assessors base their appreciation of each student upon the individual PDJs. (And some assessors base their appreciation of the course, and the course tutor, on the PDJs!)

As always, it is important that you establish the part the PDJ plays in your course. If there is no requirement for a PDJ it is nevertheless very important for you to maintain one for your own use. It can be extremely valuable to you, and you will be glad at the end of the course that you disciplined yourself both to start and sustain it. (This is an area where your family can be of great help. Establish the PDJ *and* the habit to taking the family through it every couple of weeks. This will help to establish a shared understanding of your course and of your problems and triumphs. Your family will, in short, act as your conscience. They will be the Jiminy Cricket to your Pinocchio. (With any luck *your nose will grow* every time you lie saying that you "intended to update the PDJ, but have been too busy".)

VALUE OF THE PDJ

1. A structured record of the course is maintained. You will be able to access your material easily and quickly. This is of great benefit when working on assignments, at revision time, and also in *your day to day work*.

2. Your personal development will be recorded. Looking back you will not be blinded by a coloured imagination over how things were. You will be able to see how you felt about the course, your fellow students, yourself. You will be able to follow your progress and, to some extent, measure the changes that have occurred.

3. You will be able to demonstrate to everybody interested and with a right to know, exactly how much work you have done, what you have covered and the success that you have achieved.

This can be especially important when you are asked "How good a CMS did you get?" This is a normal question from employers — your sponsoring boss will definitely want to know.

4. You will be able to show that you have planned, monitored and controlled a significant part of your personal development over a substantial period. These are all attributes of major importance in management.

5. You will help to secure your pass, especially if the PDJ is an assessed part of the course. (If it isn't, you can make sure that the assessor knows of it, and sees it if he or she wishes. It can only increase your chances of passing.)

You have to maintain some record of your course, anyway. So why not structure it in a form from which you will derive maximum benefit?

The PDJ will be confidential to you and perhaps your course tutor, unless you choose otherwise. It is not a public document. Thus you are free to make whatever pertinent comments you wish, knowing that they are solely to help in your personal development.

CONTENT OF THE PDJ

Your course tutor may very well set down clear guidelines. These must, obviously, be followed. If no such guidelines exist then follow these:

Personal Development Journal

1. Write your objectives for your PDJ very carefully. Review them regularly over a two week period at the beginning of the course. Aim to reduce them to clear succinct English. The course shape and feel will be developing at the same time and you will be able to refine your objectives over time. There is no hurry, so don't rush the job.

   Your objectives should read something like:

   This personal development journal exists to show in a structured form the progress of .... whilst on the CMS course at .... Centre.

   It will be a continuing record from which it will be possible, throughout the course and after, to assess personal learning and personal development. It will serve as a continuing source of reference material for at least a year after the course finishes.

2. Use a new A4 lever arch file, with dividers. Usually a two ring file is best as two hole punches are easily found. You can carry a small one around with you as part of your standard kit. (Thus handouts and notes can be filed straight into the PDJ when issued.)

3. Choose a positive colour and name your file in a neat dignified way. Avoid jazzy files and never doodle on your PDJ — it must be seen to be a piece of a manager's equipment.

4. Secure your course programme into the inside front cover. You will then have all the key dates, especially assignment dates, immediately to hand.

5. Assign the front section for current material. Do not file straight into the body of the PDJ, otherwise you will keep everything, regardless of value.

6. As part of your revision practice (Chapter 5) review the current material, notate it as needed, and file it into the body of the PDJ.

141

Discard everything that is if no value (rough classroom notes, for example). Maintain separate back-up filing for material of general interest.

7. Sectionalise the PDJ to match the topic areas of your course and include a section for self-analysis.

8. Add to the material issued by tutors. An active interest in general and specific newspapers and magazines will generate much that is relevant and which you will wish to share with your buddies and perhaps with the class as a whole. Television or radio material should be written up, briefly; always quote the source and date.

The PDJ should be a reflection of your personality; of your interests; of your developing abilities. It should contain every significant fact and experience that comes your way and it should be easy to read. Simplify anything which is too involved (but file the original in back-up, with a reference in the PDJ). Be sure that you record the humour of the course and the tragedies, as well as the factual items.

9. Include all individual and group assignments, together with your comments in both logical and emotional terms.

*When you analyse your position regarding any content of the PDJ ensure that you check out how you **feel** before, during and after. We all operate on emotion before logic. We may know that something, some rule or procedure, is logically correct, but if we "have a bad feeling about it" we are most likely to ignore it, or to operate it as loosely as possible. It is important that you recognise this tendency in yourself — what causes it, and what prevents it — if you are to be able to manage others.*

10. When you notice that you have used something from the course at work, or in social life, record it. Record why you used it and how effective it was. (This learning may have been from a direct input, from a group assignment, from another student over

coffee, from a mixture of situation, activity and personality. Analyse where the learning came from; why it happened; what it means to you; what contribution you made, and could have made; how to learn more in the same way.)

11. Your boss will be affected by your attendance on the course. Note how he or she reacts; in particular note the content of any formal interviews you have (again, on both logical and emotional criteria). How did he or she feel? How did you feel? Before, during and after.

12. Residential weekends are a mine of data, most of which are highly relevant to your developing awareness. Be certain to note your approach to the weekend, your expectations and fears. Note what you expect from other individuals, especially those who you have little time for, or have not got to know.

    Record during and after the weekend. You may be very surprised how your perceptions of others change. A period of close involvement, under a degree of pressure, brings out both the best and the worst in people. Your group will probably change significantly over the weekend and your individual role within it will change also. You will probably come back with a very different perception of the strengths and weaknesses of your colleagues, as they will of you.

Everything mentioned above, and more, will be happening to you and around you, whether or not you record it. The discipline of you actively observing what is happening, especially in the field of inter-personal skills, will add greatly to the benefits of your course. You will find that the demands of the PDJ will be irksome at first but, if you persist, will become second nature and essential. A PDJ, well handled, is a record that achieves far more than simply documenting course content.

Long after your course is over you will have a reference source to use and you will use it. You will also have something of value that will support your moves upwards in management. Interviewers are looking for evidence of achievement, and in management they look for analytical and stickability skills (the ability to analyse a task and the strength of character to see it through to the end). The personal development journal helps to provide that evidence. As a career development tool it is worthwhile. As a personal development aid it is invaluable.

SUMMARY

➤ You will not notice the changes in yourself — but others will.

➤ It is important to be self-aware.

➤ Compare expectation with actuality. Also compare in hindsight.

➤ Involve your family.

➤ Build a lasting record that is also a source of *useful* information.

➤ Your personal development journal is a piece of manager's equipment. Treat it as such.

➤ Comment in both logical and emotional terms.

YOUR PDJ IS PART OF A FOUNDATION ON WHICH TO DEVELOP YOUR CAREER.

Chapter 12
The Project

The project is an essential part of most general management courses. It is built into the course for several very important reasons but in some cases the objectives are not made clear to the students. The result is that the project can loom upon the horizon to spoil the enjoyment of an otherwise very happy course.

Why do you have to complete a project?

Because, simply, it is a very effective way for you to learn by undertaking an investigatory management exercise of some importance. It is an exercise that uses the skills you have learned from a range of topic areas.It is an opportunity for you to learn through doing. (Understanding comes through use.) It is also, very importantly, an opportunity for your employer to see the quality of your work.

To quote from the rationale for a general management course project:

> *The project is an important element of the overall assessment of the course. It accounts for 150 marks out of a total of 700. Its purpose is:*
>
> *1. To demonstrate the ability of the project writer to employ systematic knowledge and analysis:*
>
> *1.1 to investigate and diagnose a real managerial problem;*
>
> *1.2 to devise and evaluate alternative solutions to the problem;*

1.3 to produce practical recommendations for (management) action, and indicate method(s) of implementation where appropriate;

1.4 to establish control criteria as appropriate.

2. To integrate skills and knowledge gained during the course with the "everyday" activities at the workplace.

3. To provide incentive to the student for a sustained piece of work leading to part of the assessment process.

Your project will have been established for purposes very similar to these. Discover exactly what they are. Do not embark on a piece of work that is going to take a considerable amount of your time without checking thoroughly that you know why you are doing it, what it is expected to achieve and how it will be evaluated. Only after you have answers to these questions should you concern yourself with details like length, structure, style.

Most management projects are undertaken for, and with the prior agreement of, the students' senior management. But a project is also one of the assessed components of the course. This means that your work must meet the needs both of your management and your course.

You *must* write a management report. A report is most effective when targeted upon a single person. Your moderator will be the final arbiter of quality and so it is for him or her that you should be writing.

He or she is external to your work, thus you will need to introduce him or her to the business/market, and the organisation in which the investigation has been carried out. Section 1 becomes "Introduction" in many projects. This need to explain background detail is a very good discipline that will prevent you cutting corners.

Your management will most probably turn straight to your recommendations, believing that they know the background from which you are reporting. If they are wrong — if you want to report an inconsistency between their belief and yours, then you will have to make it very clear in your recommendations (or, perhaps, in your conclusions).

TIME TRAP

Beware of falling into the time trap. It is very easy to under-estimate the time needed to complete a project. Your course programme will allow time for the project but don't be lulled into false security.

Most of the project work has to be done in your own time and so the course weeks allowed make assumptions about how much time you will devote to the work. The benchmark is usually the best estimate of time needed by the most efficient student, working on a straightforward project. It is seldom realistic — and is most unlikely to apply to you.

The safest solution is to start the broad planning of your project as early as possible. Just as soon as you feel that you have the rest of the course under control. Planning, at this early stage, means thinking through the areas in which you would like to work and identifying a specific area within these that your employer is interested in knowing more about. Try not to get landed with a project that someone else chooses for you and try not to get committed to a project in a sensitive area of your firm. Investigations involving internal security or cost/profit figures are very sensitive.

Whatever employers say at project planning stage they always fight shy of giving students access to sensitive material when it is actually asked for! This is not surprising if you think about it, but employers generally have no idea just how searching a management project can be and they allow a student to start with every intention of support. You must not allow your project to be cancelled (or changed significantly) halfway through by your employer pulling out, so do be very careful in selecting/accepting your project topic.

TUTOR TRAP

Project tutoring requires special skills and, as with every skill, some people have it developed to a finer degree than others. Beware the tutor who says "Let me know when you need me". How do you know when help is needed? By the time you realise it is too late!

Preferably locate a good project tutor for yourself. In most cases this can be done; it is certainly worth trying since otherwise you will be *allocated* a tutor and possibly fall into the tutor trap.

What you need is a tutor with whom you are compatible because you will work together over several months. You also need one with a reputation for bringing project students through to success on time. Tutors' reputations are easy to discover. There are always students around from other courses; you will know someone from last year's course; the tutors themselves will tell you if you ask gently or tactfully and at the right time. (One to one over coffee is a good method.) You can check projects from previous courses; the tutor's name is usually mentioned in the acknowledgements. (Previous projects are usually available, often from the library.)

Don't go for the "Mr Nice Guy"; go for the person who has a reputation for helping students to complete projects of a good standard, to time. If you like him or her that's a bonus. Incidentally, one doesn't have to be a subject expert to be a good project tutor. What you need is a person who is good at helping students with projects. That comes down, essentially, to an insistence on careful planning and an ability to ask penetrating questions.

Can you ask for your own tutor? Of course you can. If you are planning ahead, and you should be, you can arrange to bump into the tutor of choice and ask for a chat. Say that you are beginning to plan your project and you'd be glad of a piece of advice. (You must have something specific to be advised about.) If you get good advice and you get along, you'll have made an impact. Use your judgement about how and when to broach the subject, but at the right time make a direct request — "would you be willing to tutor my project?" It is very flattering to be asked and tutors get a kick out of helping students achieve good project results. Once provisional agreement has been reached you can ask "how do we arrange this, please?" Often you will be told to make a formal request for your project tutor to the course tutor (a supporting word will go to the course tutor from your project tutor). A final word of advice — it is best not to make too much noise about this. Softly softly is the best approach. Centres couldn't run if everyone went around setting up their own private arrangements!

Once you are authorised to start on your project and you have a tutor you must get into the outline planning stage. We shall look at the planning of the content in a moment; let us now concentrate upon the overall strategy.

PROJECT STRATEGY

Assuming you have from the end of November to the end of April to complete the project, you can establish an outline calendar:

1 December	Formal commencement of project.
15 December	Centre closes for Christmas vacation.
4 January	Spring term commences.
2 April	Centre closes for Easter vacation.
9/12 April	Easter weekend.
26 April	Centre re-opens after Easter.
30 April	Deadline for submission.

There are certain blocks in this time plan that you must take into account:

1. When the centre is closed for the Christmas and Easter vacations.

2. You will not do any work on the project over Christmas or Easter. (Be honest!)

3. There is, in this example, one centre week before the deadline. This can only be used for final project checking by the tutor and for copying and binding your work.

4. Between 12 and 25 April you have time for the final typescript to be prepared and for proof-reading. (Do not under-estimate the time a good typist needs to produce a project report that is very well set out and that will be a credit to your work.)

5. Your actual deadline for completion of work on the project (as opposed to the presentation of the project) appears, therefore, to be 7 April. But you will have to allow your tutor a week to go through your final draft and you will have to set up a final meeting to take the tutors' comments. So your actual deadline for completion comes back to 1 April.

    You have calculated that the project time is one month less than the course programme says it is!

6. Obviously you must have your project plan agreed by your tutor before he or she goes off for Christmas, so that sets up a first reporting date. Then you need a second report date early in January to keep you on your toes. (Otherwise the vacation will slip by and three weeks will be lopped off your schedule.)

    You also need a mid-term report date, again to ensure that you are motivated to keep on with the work. Finally, you need a session after the tutor has read your final draft.

    These are the report times you need. Your tutor may want to see you (or hear from you) more often. Whatever — you must establish, with your tutor, a time plan that shows clearly what you intend to achieve and by when.

7. Your outline project plan will therefore look something like this:

October	First thoughts on topic area. Check availability and quality of tutors.
November	Check with employer over exact topic area. Rough out a project proposal, including draft terms of reference.
1 December	Project proposals to course tutor. Project tutor appointed.
8 December	Terms of reference agreed with tutor.
15 December	Project plan agreed by tutor.
4 January	Work on body of project commences.
15 January	Progress review no.1.
20 February	Progress review no.2.
26 March	Final draft to tutor.
1 April	Final review.
13 April	Final draft to typist.
20 April	Typescript received for proof reading.
22 April	Corrected manuscript to typist.
27 April	Bound project(s) available for final check.
30 April	Project submitted.

Note: This time plan allows only three days' slippage. Do not under estimate the time your typist will need to do a good job for you.

You will see that there is very little time for the actual work *you* need to do.

8. **Cardinal principles**

(a) Do not be deceived by the time that apparently is available.

(b) Start your project just as soon as you are able.

(c) Do not undertake too large a task.

(d) Check, at the beginning, that you will have access to *all* the information you will need.

(e) Remember — you will have assignments to complete, course work to maintain, a job to do and a private life to lead, in addition to the project.

PROJECT STAGES

There are *nine* stages to project completion:

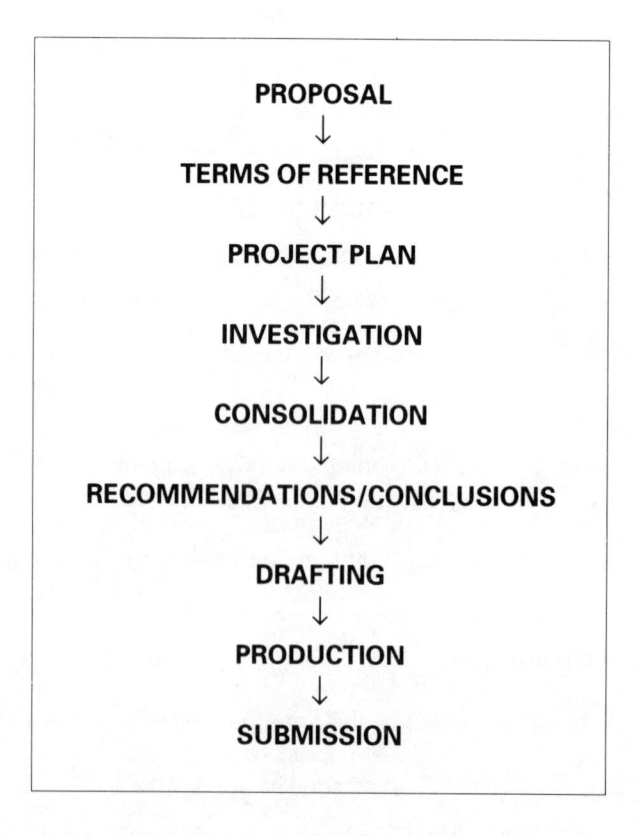

PROPOSAL
↓
TERMS OF REFERENCE
↓
PROJECT PLAN
↓
INVESTIGATION
↓
CONSOLIDATION
↓
RECOMMENDATIONS/CONCLUSIONS
↓
DRAFTING
↓
PRODUCTION
↓
SUBMISSION

The proposal

This should be a very short description of the intended project. Sometimes a special form is supplied, sometimes not. Either way it is essential for you to formalise your first thoughts in writing.

Don't try to be too precise at this stage. Your aim in the proposal should be to make clear:

(a) why the project is proposed;

(b) what benefits it will bring to its sponsor;

(c) if special circumstances will apply (confidentiality, perhaps).

You should also indicate *who* you are, the *course* you are taking and the *date* for completion. Include a *working title*. Indicate the main area(s) of your proposed investigation.

At this stage you should have a first draft of your proposed terms of reference.

PROJECT PLAN — Example (from a student employed in education).

PROJECT PROPOSAL

> *Name: Chris Knight   DATE: 26.11.9_*
> *Course: NEBSM General (Course reference 7059)*
> *Title: Recruitment of students to NEBSM Courses at XXX Centre*
>
> *It is proposed to investigate the sources of recruitment and methods of selection of students on the NEBSM course at XXX Centre. The aim of the project is to improve the quality and quantity of students recruited.*
>
> *The project will make clear recommendations concerning the cost-effective recruitment of students to the benefit of employers, students and the centre.*

No attempt will be made to assess the quality of the course itself. (This is under constant review by the course board.)

*Completion date: 30.4.9_*

A project proposal should be a short document. Its purpose is to allow others to understand what is in your mind. It will help in the selection of a project tutor (especially important if you will need the help of a financial specialist, for instance). It will be a basis on which your employer can agree (or not) to the project going ahead. It will be the basis for your terms of reference. It is the key to the success of the whole project!

Terms of reference

This is a formal statement that sets out clearly and unambiguously the objective of the investigation, its scope and parameters, the areas in which you will work and an indication of the type of recommendations you will make. Once agreed, the terms of reference must be complied with *exactly* and so it is crucial that they are correct. (They can be changed later, but only with the greatest difficulty and for the most compelling of reasons.)

You will find specific terms of reference invaluable as you work through the project. In February you will be thankful that you have them. The time spent in November and December is an investment that you must make. Why? Because there is another project trap — the tangent trap.

THE TANGENT TRAP

The tangent trap is waiting for the unwary. It is like being in an enchanted forest. There you are, happily trundling away on the tracks mapped out by your project plan. Then you notice a lovely new path going off to one side. It has bigger flowers and more juicy looking berries. The danger of turning off is that you are going into unmapped forest. Will there be other side tracks? Will you follow them? Will you ever get back to your mapped area? Will you ever complete your journey?

Your terms of reference are your goal and your plan is your map through your project. Think ahead, include only what you must have, be ruthless. Beware the thought "It will be interesting to investigate this area"! Is it of value to the project? Does it fall within the terms of reference?

Be sure to specifically exclude any unneeded areas that are sensitive, confidential, too big to handle, better taken as a separate project. (If an area is needed and it is sensitive or confidential then a method of access and reporting has to be found *before* the project starts.)

The most important part of a project tutor's job is done when good terms of reference are established.

TERMS OF REFERENCE — EXAMPLE

Recruitment and selection of students to the NEBSM Course at XXX Centre

TERMS OF REFERENCE

1. *To investigate and recommend a methodology to optimise satisfactory student recruitment to the NEBSM Course at XXX Centre.*
2. *"Satisfactory student recruitment" is defined as:*

    "Location, recruitment and selection of students capable of sustaining a NEBSM Certificate course of study."
3. *Exclusions: academic content, teaching methodology, academic assessment criteria.*

You will notice the influence of the project tutor in these terms of reference. Your target achievement is established beyond any doubt; the most obvious tangent traps are specifically excluded. Everything is a tangent trap if it is not in the terms of reference. The point of exclusions is to reassure employers that sensitive areas will not be investigated and to show the assessor that the project will be of manageable size. In this case it would be most inappropriate to investigate areas under the control, and affecting the career, of your course tutor!

Note that where the student wrote "increase the quantity and quality of students" the terms of reference say "optimise satisfactory student recruitment". (Optimise means "make the best compromise". Thus the tutor-aided terms of reference are saying "don't let's go for sheer volume, we need quality as well as quantity, and let us be careful not to recruit students who are over-qualified for NEBSM".)

The project plan

We have dealt with the outline project plan earlier. You need a clear understanding, in writing, of what you need to achieve, how and by when. In other words, clear objectives for each stage of your project and some detail of how to achieve each: a clear path to follow.

As with every plan you will find that keeping to it exactly is impossible. Yet without an original plan you will have no idea how far from target you are, how much extra work has to be squeezed in and how much of a set-back results from an unforeseen situation.

What do you do if you are scheduled to interview a manager during the first week of February and he goes sick? Have you other work you can get on with? Have you slippage in your plan? Have you an alternative way to obtain the information you need?

The project plan should set out the exact shape the final project will take. You won't know the detailed contents of each section but you should establish a title for each section and indicate its content. You should know the running order.

Once you have the shape of the whole project firm and in writing you

The Project

will find it easy to work on several sections at once. This may sound difficult, but actually it is routine once the original thinking is complete.

A film crew does not travel to a location, Venice say, and film the first scene for a movie then fly off to Mexico City for the next scene, come back to Florence for scene three and return to Venice for scene four. What the director actually does is work out what scenes he needs to film in each location, which actors and crew are needed, if any particular time of year is needed for a particular scene, and so on. Then he schedules accordingly. Actors, especially those in supporting roles are used as cost effectively as possible, which means that scenes in which they appear are filmed at one time. It is the film editor's job to cut the film so that the scenes are put together in the sequence for which the director has been aiming.

In just the same way you should be working out the content for each section of your project, deciding the sources you need to tap and setting up your work schedule accordingly.

You will find that data obtained from one source can be combined with data from others, and that some will go into section one, some into three and some into four. Thus you are working on your whole project at one time. You are *not* working through from section one onwards. (We shall come back to this area under "Drafting".)

Your project plan must be individual to your project's needs. The plan used by Chris Knight on the NEBSM Course at XXX Centre came out as:

Project outline:

    Cover   — To centre requirement.

    1st sheet — Title of project/of course/student name.

    2nd sheet — Terms of reference.

    3rd sheet — Acknowledgements of help received.

    Contents — with page numbers (produced last).

Qualify in Management

     — NB: To be strictly accurate "pages" start with Section 1: "Sheets" in the front of your project need not be numbered, but if they are you should use roman numerals.

Section 1 — Introduction/background/rationale for project.

Section 2 — Analysis of achievement — student entry/retention/pass rate/present situation.

Section 3 — Catchment area of centre/of course.

Section 4 — Competing centres/courses.

Section 5 — Employer and student requirements; success of centre/course in meeting these.

Section 6 — Recruitment/selection/evaluation of alternative methods.

Section 7 — Conclusions.

Section 8 — Recommendations.

Appendices — As required (may need to include a glossary).

A clear way to present your plan is shown opposite.

Investigation

It may be that you, and perhaps your boss, already know what you want the project to prove. The objective is often to make a case for achievement of some objective (a staff increase perhaps) but this will often be hidden under a neutral title such as "An examination of staff workloads in XYZ Department". Perhaps you truly do not know what the results of the project "should" be. Either way, to make the case, whatever it is, you must have evidence. You must show that this is factual evidence, that can be relied upon and that it is valid in the circumstances of your report. *You must show that this is factual evidence.* **Show.**

You *must* enter the investigation with an open mind (or as open a

PROJECT TIME PLAN

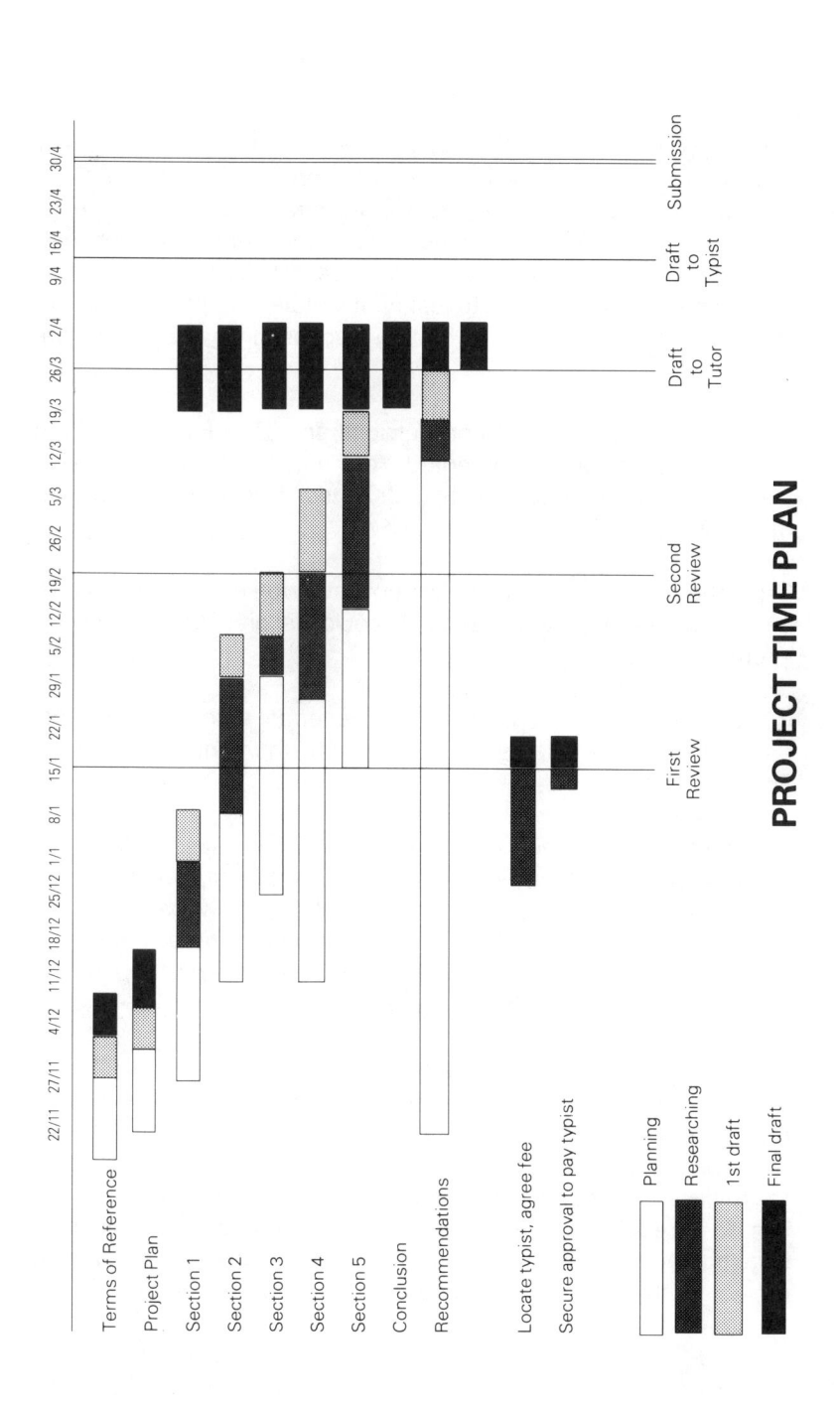

| | 22/11 | 27/11 | 4/12 | 11/12 | 18/12 | 25/12 | 1/1 | 8/1 | 15/1 | 22/1 | 29/1 | 5/2 | 12/2 | 19/2 | 26/2 | 5/3 | 12/3 | 19/3 | 26/3 | 2/4 | 9/4 | 16/4 | 23/4 | 30/4 |

Terms of Reference
Project Plan
Section 1
Section 2
Section 3
Section 4
Section 5
Conclusion
Recommendations
Locate typist, agree fee
Secure approval to pay typist

First Review — Second Review — Draft to Tutor — Draft to Typist — Submission

Legend:
- Planning
- Researching
- 1st draft
- Final draft

mind as you can manage). What you need at this stage are *facts*. If you try to justify an already decided position you will miss facts, or get them out of perspective. You will be distracted by your own bias. Thus your project will not be a neutral summary of the position with a rationale for action. It will be, and be seen to be, a biased report from someone with a case to justify. It will be very much harder to implement and an easy target for those opposed to your recommendations.

It is not sufficient just to report opinions; the basis for each opinion must be checked and documented. You should continually be asking "why?" "Why do you believe that, Mr Jones?" "Why do you say that, Mrs Smith?"

Often the person you interview will not have worked out why. It could be hunch based on experience. It could be prejudice, rumour or internal politics.

It could be sheer hard fact. You must *penetrate* with your investigation and root out the facts that support the argument or the feeling. Then present both:

It is widely felt in the Department of Administrative Affairs that students released for a NEBSM Course are an unjustified drain on company resources. The facts, however, clearly show that of the nine students released for NEBSM courses in the last three years, eight are still with the department and have been promoted to departmental management posts. (See Appendix D.)

In the example quoted there is a need to set out the details of each student in the appendix. There is also a need to make a note for your recommendations. There is a possible tangent trap here. If your terms of reference do not permit you to investigate internal feelings about the release of students (and Chris Knight's do not) then the most you can do is recommend that the reason for the negative feelings be investigated and a report to management made. It is a job for another project student, or for your manager, not for you at this time.

Consolidation

As you progress you will find that your file grows bulky. You will also develop an overall feel for the project. You will be able to relate sections together and understand how the project interlocks and inter-relates. You will come to certain views based on your in-depth understanding.

Beware! Your readers will not have lived with your project as you have. They have to be taken carefully into and through the project; and helped to understand what is so clear to you.

This is the time to re-appraise the structure of the project. How can you make it simple for your manager to understand? Will it be more effective if you add a summary at the front, or would that give an impression of shallowness? Could your material be better used if the contents of each section were altered from your original plan? (A plan is a guide to action made at a moment in time in the light of data then available. As fresh data becomes available it is right that plans are re-appraised and changed if necessary.)

Do you need a section titled "Conclusions" (which we shall deal with in the next section)?

Recommendations and conclusions

Recommendations are the purpose of the project. A management report that does not come up with clear and specific recommendations is useless.

The test of a good recommendation is that it sells itself: a senior manager will understand it and be able to take action directly from it. There can be only three reactions to well written recommendations.

1. Agreed, take action.
2. Do not agree, take no action.
3. Looks interesting, but I need more data.

Reactions 1 and 2 come from managers who are on top of their jobs and who have a detailed knowledge of the area of your project. They will immediately register the validity of the recommendation and hardly need to go through the arguments that you have so carefully assembled. If they trust your judgement, and the recommendation is clear and specific, they will be able to initiate action. (Once the action is agreed, however, the manager responsible for implementation will find your work invaluable.)

Reaction 3 comes when you open an area that is new or novel. Then the manager will want to follow through your arguments, evaluate your evidence, perhaps do some investigation of his or her own. These might be the most valuable recommendations of all since they are innovative.

There is a fourth reaction — "My word! What did we release this person for! What a waste of time!" This comes when your thinking and/or presentation is sloppy! It can so easily be avoided, especially with the help of a tutor.

A recommendation must be clear, specific and indicate a timescale. Indicate the degree of urgency, if this is appropriate. (Not everything can be done at once and some actions are dependent upon others being completed first.) A good recommendation would be:

> The NEBSM promotional pack should be re-designed within three months. It should include:
>
> (a) details of the XXX Centre NEBSM;
>
> (b) the fee structure;
>
> (c) the NEBSM brochure;
>
> (d) an application form (Appendix H);
>
> (e) an addressed, but not stamped, envelope of the correct size for the return of the application.

Always direct the reader to supporting evidence or, in this case, prepared material (Appendix H). Do not expect the reader to find his or her own way around your project. Think through your recommendations "...addressed but not stamped...", "...envelope of the correct size...".

A bad recommendation would be:

The NEBSM promotional pack should be re-designed.

The body of the project will be narrative. It will tell the story, as it were. Supporting the narrative will be appendices. These carry the detailed facts that are necessary for reference as one reads the narrative but which not every reader will want to turn to. All of this must be written in a neutral, third person style. You are reporting facts, not commenting on them. You must not allow your personal feelings into the project *except possibly in the Conclusions.*

The whole point and purpose of your project is to make recommendations to management and to set out actions that could be taken to improve the efficiency and/or effectiveness of the operation. You will come across areas in which you wish to make recommendations as you work through the months. Write these down, in rough, at the time. Put them into your notes. You will be surprised how many recommendations you will come up with. (Students who write their project and then go through it looking for recommendations commonly find them very hard to identify. The time to do it is while the idea is fresh in the mind.)

Do not try to polish recommendations at this time. Simply note them carefully and file them under "Recommendations" in your ring binder. Don't even check to see if you have noted the same recommendation more than once. Include recommendations based on evaluation, on hunch, and on intuition. In due course you will go through them all, decide which are valid, determine that there is evidence in the narrative to support each, and put them into a logical sequence. That is the time to refine and polish them.

If a fact is not included in the narrative it cannot be used in the Conclusions nor the Recommendations.

It is perfectly valid to recommend "no action", or "continue without change". If that is what the facts show, that is what you recommend.

Many project reports commence the recommendations section with just this point. If your recommendation is that current practice should not change, then say so. It is welcome news for managers to read that something in their operation is running successfully and should not be changed.

On the other hand it is very difficult to cause an organisation to terminate an operation which has long been established.

Robert Townsend, in "Further Up the Organisation" describes how difficult it is to find a manager who is willing to close down an operation. He recommends bringing in someone, a retired chief executive in his example, to manage a new project. He will be dedicated, says Townsend, and only be willing to devote time to it, when he could be doing something else, whilst it still interests him. Thus he will fight for it whilst it is viable, and close it down when it isn't. For many managers in line posts, wanting to develop a career, there is a need to keep a project going even it is losing their organisation money, position or reputation. Very few feel able to report "This isn't going to work. Close it down".

When recommending each change it is valuable and helpful to state not only what change(s) you recommend, but to indicate who should be responsible for making the change(s) and when.

You will gain additional credit if you highlight the main managerial, human and/or financial aspects of each recommendation, especially the anticipated benefits.

Conclusions

This is the one place in the project in which you have the opportunity

The Project

to include your own personal observations. (The whole of the project will normally be written in third person and you will not be able to include your personal views directly.)

Not every project has a Conclusions section. You will only need one if you want to express an underlying opinion, or feeling, that has built up as you have worked through the project, but which you have not been able to quantify. Perhaps it is outside your terms of reference or is simple hunch or intuition, but you feel it strongly enough for it to be reported.

You may like to include a brief statement of any particular benefit or learning experience that you have gained from completing the project.

A typical Conclusion may read (in part):

> *The NEBSM Course at XXX Centre is hard work, but enjoyable. This is due mainly to the efforts of the individual lecturers since there is no system of planning and control. Underlying the whole of this investigation has been a feeling of happy chaos, shown most clearly in the air of casualness which permeates the entire course. This is extremely hard to quantify, but it is a prevailing attitude that is obvious to those exposed to it and which reduces the effectiveness of the course overall. There is a need for a long term view to be taken, and detailed plans actioned, if the course is to justify its full potential.*

Drafting

A ring binder is the most effective way to manage your papers. Set it up with dividers so that each section is identified. Build up the data for each section as you go.

Draft the project section by section, but do allow time for a final re-write. This is when you go through the rough draft of the finalised project to check that the material is in the most appropriate sequence and to ensure that your style is consistent. Otherwise you will change style from section to section and from page to page. (This book was not written front to back; each chapter was drafted when the data was to hand. It was then revised thoroughly, and a final draft submitted to the publisher. The sub-editor then went through it in great detail, corrected very many errors and improved the style. A book is a collaboration between author and editor much as a project is a collaboration between student and tutor.)

You will build up the appendices as you carry out your investigation. Make certain that there is a need for each appendix and that each one is as brief and as clear as possible.

Ensure that each appendix is cross-referenced from the narrative.

Weight does not make a good project, nor does length. Clarity, directness, good presentation, completeness and clear recommendations based upon facts are the essentials.

A current project being carried out for a fee is occupying six months of a colleague's time. His report will run to some 250 pages, but the summary of main points and recommendations will occupy a maximum of eight pages.

These eight pages will be placed at the front of the report because the senior manager who briefed him stated that the directors of the company only make time to read short documents.

(To get to an eight page action document from a six month investigation is not easy, but it is what the client requires. The supporting rationale, the other 242 pages, will be used by management only if the directors approve the recommendations.)

At the drafting stage you are aiming initially to turn out a document that is structured in the most effective way, that has every section in place and that is as complete as possible. (You may have yet to complete work on one of the appendices, for example, but there will be a page in place saying what the appendix will contain and when it will be ready. At the time of drafting this chapter there was a blank page in place for the detailed time plan when it was ready.)

The Project

Your first draft goes to your tutor for comment. Individuals differ in their preferences, so check whether to submit it section by section or the whole thing at one time. By all means get an independent person to read through at this stage — not the manager the project is being written for. An independent person will pick up on your grammatical errors and tell you if the style is interesting. It is important that the project is readable and that it sustains the interest of the reader(s) throughout.

What style of presentation you use is for your company, centre and tutor to advise. The project must be a management report but there are several report styles for you to choose from. Pick the one you are most comfortable with if you have a choice, obviously!

When you have your tutor's comments you can get down to your final draft. This is the one from which a typist or wp operator will produce the project you will submit. You do not want the contents page typed at this time, and the appendices should be referred to without their letters. Get the typist to leave spaces. (You will probably find that your appendices have got out of order as you have been working with the final draft; also you may well make several references to the same appendix. This can only be sorted after the narrative is finalised.)

Note: After typing you have the opportunity for minor corrections only, not for re-writes. The temptation to re-write after the final draft is a serious tangent trap that you must avoid.

When you have the typescript you must go through it carefully for errors. Mark these in soft pencil, very lightly, and mark each page that has an error — turn it sideways, or use a "Post It" note.

The appendices must be distinguished from each other, and from the narrative. Usually, appendices are labelled alphabetically and the project sections numerically. As you read through for errors you will come to an appendix reference. Mark the typescript A, and mark the appendix A also. The next appendix reference is labelled B and so on. Do this carefully and you will have the appendices in order, and correctly labelled.

169

Give the whole project back to the typist, with the appendices, so the corrections can be made, the appendices identified and page numbers added. It is now possible to type the contents page, since the page numbers are finalised.

Production

This should be a routine process but it takes time. Find a typist who is experienced in this area. It is a skill that only relatively few possess. (Previous projects will give you pointers. Choose one or two that you like and find out from their authors who typed them.)

Do not endanger your efforts with a sub-standard presentation. Check carefully for spelling and punctuation errors. Presentation is crucial: first impressions count, so make certain that your document will create a favourable impression instantly. A good job will not come cheap but it will be efficient and most effective.

Very exceptionally and for a specific purpose, it is possible to deviate from these basic rules. But only deviate after taking a conscious decision that is justified by the firm belief that your project will benefit in management decision terms (it will be more credible). A student in a centre of art and design will probably need to use an imaginative style and presentation. Students on a retail management course may need to be specially creative when dealing with such topics as in-store merchandising or high street location. Otherwise there are basic rules to follow.

Presentation

1. Type/print the project.

2. Ensure the typewriter/printer has a new ribbon and a clean typeface.

3. Double space.

4. Allow a one and a half inch margin on the left and one inch on the right (to allow for binding).

5. Use crisp white paper.

6. Never cramp the work — allow too much rather than too little space.

7. Bind horizontal diagrams, etc, from the *top*. (The project is turned clockwise for the material to be read.)

8. Number sections using whichever method is appropriate to you.

9. Use dividers if this will help the reader.

10. Appendices go at the back and in the order they first appear in the narrative.

11. Use a good photocopier and insist on clean copies.

12. Bind so that the project opens easily. (If it is very large, bind the appendices as a separate volume.)

The addition of a transparent sheet over the normal cover adds a quality that helps "sell" your work.

Follow your tutor's guidance on how and where to title the project. Some prefer the name and title on the outside cover and first sheet, some on the first sheet only.

If the project is confidential then label it *very clearly* on the first sheet and submit it in a sealed envelope.

Submission

1. Submit to time and present the number of copies called for.

2. Submit to a person, not to a post tray or an office desk.
3. Note in your diary to whom you submitted and at what time.
4. Keep an extra copy for yourself, over and above those required by the centre and by work. (Projects have been lost and the risk is not worth the cost of prevention.)

SUMMARY

▶ Find out exactly why you are required to undertake the project.

▶ Beware the *time trap;* plan and control your time.

▶ Avoid the *tutor trap;* organise yourself the best tutor available.

▶ Don't fall into the *tangent trap.* Set good terms of reference and follow them.

▶ Manage your project:

  set a strategy;

  plan detailed objectives for content, time and presentation;

  establish reporting dates;

  monitor progress;

  complete to time;

  work on the *whole* project. Build it as one entity.

▶ Facts are essential. Opinion points the need for factual investigation.

▶ Recommendations must be supported by *facts* in the narrative.

▶ Appendices support and extend the facts included in the narrative.

▶ Write in the third person (except possibly in the conclusions).

- Recommendations are for action. Present them so that they are clear, complete and detailed.

- Expect your manager to read *only* your recommendations, Your project stands or falls by them.

- Submit to time, to a person and note in your diary when and to whom.

- Keep a spare copy.

MAKE IT EASY TO READ AND EASY FOR A MANAGER TO INITIATE ACTION.

Chapter 13
The Residential Weekend

Many management courses contain a "residential element". Usually this is a weekend, especially for courses run one day a week over several months. We shall use the term "weekend" as it is so much more attractive than "element". The principles of a "weekend" hold whether the period is mid-week or at a weekend.

One or more weekends are built into most management courses, partly to increase the number of teaching hours available, but mostly because a weekend is such a valuable learning experience.

A weekend can be planned into a course early to establish a group dynamic or occur at the mid-point or two-thirds of the way through to consolidate learning.

The course tutor will position the weekend and plan its content to meet specific objectives. A weekend placed early will involve management games and exercises which help course members get to know each other; establish individual strengths and weaknesses; build a healthy attitude and a sense of group identity.

A course taking its weekend later will already have an established identity, its personality will have formed and the tutors will know the individuals that comprise the group. They will use the weekend to consolidate learning: exercises and/or management games are likely to be longer and more complex. The whole weekend may be devoted to a single exercise which, apart from the value to the weekend itself, could not be run successfully within the limitations of centre attendance.

Some courses are structured with two weekends. It is very important to build group cohesion *and* to work through a complex management exercise. Thus two weekends, one early, one late in the course are ideal.

No matter when your weekend is placed, and no matter what its objectives are, it will be most unusual if you do not enjoy it. A well planned weekend has a tremendous effect on all who take part. It is likely to be remembered over many years.

At this point a note of caution — the intensity which weekends engender is exciting but exhausting. Students tend to stay up late and some of the tiredness that hits on the day *after* the weekend is self-engendered. It is none the less real and you will be wise to plan a light Monday. Going into class after a day at work, after a weekend, is not to be recommended!

HOW TO ENJOY YOUR WEEKEND

1. Decide that you are going to enjoy the weekend.
2. Listen carefully to the briefing.
3. Set yourself clear objectives.
4. Arrive on time.
5. Commit yourself fully.
6. Laugh and be happy!
7. Travel home carefully.

Decide you are going to enjoy the weekend because the weekend will be as good as you make it. You have no choice about attending. It is a part of the course and, whilst avoiding the weekend may be possible, it would be very silly. Those who go will generate experiences that they will share and which they will bring back with them to the weekly classes. There will be in-jokes, a form of shorthand that you will not share. You have to be there.

One weekend involved the setting up of a management structure to deal with an emergency situation that the students were to be briefed on the following day. The tutors left the students to the task of setting up their organisation but refused to give any details of the exercise however hard the students tried to find out the details. (And they tried everything up to and including bribery!)

When the problem was solved the students notified the tutors, who found the following structure prepared for them:

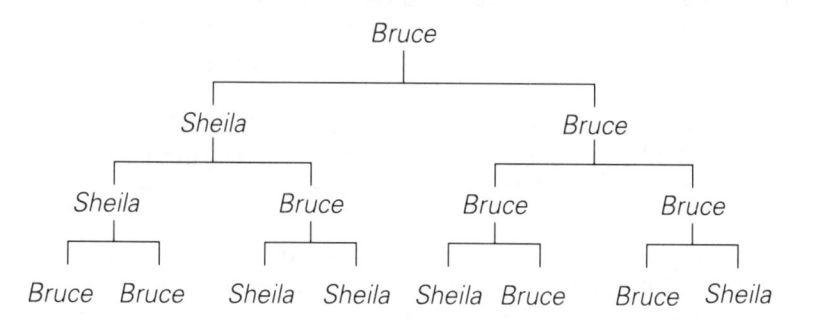

```
                        Bruce
              ┌───────────┴───────────┐
            Sheila                  Bruce
         ┌────┴────┐            ┌────┴────┐
       Sheila    Bruce        Bruce     Bruce
       ┌─┴─┐     ┌─┴─┐        ┌─┴─┐     ┌─┴─┐
     Bruce Bruce Sheila Sheila Sheila Bruce Bruce Sheila
```

A piece of good fun that was taken in the spirit intended. But for the rest of the year the Bruce/Sheila joke remained, and only those on the weekend ever understood it!

Commit yourself — go in totally. Don't hold back. Don't pre-judge. Your tutors will have planned the whole weekend very carefully (as we shall see a little later) and there will be a clear purpose underlying the programme.

One syndicate on a management weekend decided that a problem they had been set was unfair because it was too difficult. They stayed in their syndicate room and worked themselves up into a lather over the stupidity of the tutors, the course, the weekend, life itself!

It never occurred to them to consider that many other syndicates had been given the same problem over the years; that their colleagues in the next room were working to the same brief; that tutors exist to help.

When they finally called for help, as everyone else had, they were given a tutorial that showed how to solve the problem. One of the learning objectives set by the tutors was to ensure that the students learned to call for help and did not feel themselves to be self-sufficient. This particular syndicate made it very hard on themselves, but a valuable lesson was learned, both by themselves and by the other students.

Listen carefully — the weekend will be briefed ahead of time and each exercise will be briefed before it is run. The briefing may be oral or in writing. You need to understand it *before* you start!

Establish clearly, at the outset, from the course tutor or the weekend leader, whether all, or part, of the weekend is being assessed. (This is discussed in more detail towards the end of this chapter.)

Read (or listen) carefully. Ask questions. Listen to the questions from other students. Listen, especially carefully, to the answers being given. Tutors are constantly amazed by the frantic desire of students to *begin*. To rush headlong into a problem, long before it has been fully understood.

Students are divided into teams. The leader is briefed that a magazine has been accidentally torn up. Will the team please stick it back together. Sellotape is available. At the front of the room are 20" lengths of sellotape, as many as there are teams. The assumption is that each team has one length, that no more is available. But the tutor carefully does not say so.

Even knowing that 20" of tape is not enough it is common for teams to start by using an inch (a whole inch — 5% of their resources) to stick just two pieces of one page together. There are 80 pages in all!

If the leader thought the problem through, if the team asked questions, it would be seen to be an impossible task. If the tutor was approached extra sellotape would be made available. (Or by moving fast one team could steal all the tape and so be the only one able to complete the task!)

But team after team, on course after course, make the same mistakes — they do not listen, they do not understand, they do not think.

Set yourself clear objectives — the weekend is a unique chance for you to try out your management skills in safety. What is the worst that can happen? You attract some good humoured laughter. (Unless you set out to deliberately destroy the enjoyment of others, of course.)

You don't have to "win" the weekend in terms of other people's expectations. You do have to succeed in your own estimation. To make a success of a weekend decide what you want from it. If you want to try out a different management style, then adopt it for the weekend. See how it works. If you are never creative, never take risks, deliberately force yourself to try. So what if you are not successful in "winning" the game? Your true objective should be to make yourself a better manager. Others have weaknesses too, but are they trying to improve, or are they restricting themselves to work they already know they can do?

A high flying, very successful buddy group should have come top in a management game run over a weekend. To everybody's surprise they came out with the worst results at de-briefing on the Sunday morning.

But they were not unhappy; far from it, they were positively radiant. At the de-brief in the centre the truth came out. They were aware of their strengths and made a decision to try a different approach. They saw the weekend as a learning experience, and they wrote personal learning objectives. In their own terms they were successful. They achieved their objectives and they did no harm to anybody.

If you decide to set your own learning objectives there are two things you must do:

1. Put them in writing before the weekend.

2. Tell the course tutor what you intend, and why. (It may be that, whilst a good idea, it is not appropriate on this occasion.)

Arrival on time is not only courteous, it has practical advantages. You can:

(a) have the best chance of a parking space;

(b) locate your room and settle in;

(c) shower and change;

(d) investigate the hotel or training centre;

(e) be relaxed and comfortable at the pre-course briefing.

If you can't possibly arrive on time then don't try. Rushing sets you off to a bad start. You are flustered and unlikely to do yourself justice. Get a message to the course tutor at the venue, also one direct to your buddy if you can. Arrangements will be made for a meal to be kept for you (if necessary) and the course programme will be adjusted so you can slip in with as little bother as possible. (Tutors are used to accommodating latecomers. It is appreciated that your job must come first.)

Laugh and be happy needs no explaining. The best results come from happy people and happiness is infectious. When it gets tough, look for the brighter side. There always is one but it may be hard to find.

No weekend exercise is sufficiently important to cause you stress and suffering. If this is about to happen call for your tutor; you are doing something wrong!

The Residential Weekend

A syndicate on a weekend found itself in deep trouble one Saturday afternoon. By misreading the original brief on Friday evening they had reached a point from which there was no way forward. They had to go back and re-work their material. It could have been very depressing and many groups would have collapsed into bitterness.

This group didn't. They looked for a solution. It was there, of course. It always is, if one looks. The tutors were approached and a crash recovery instituted. By accepting a tutor as a working member of the group — not as its leader — they were able to recover the situation and hit their deadline. The learning was not in the exercise, of course. It was in the acceptance of the need for help and the ability to call for and use it.

Travel home carefully applies most importantly if you are driving. A weekend will build up your adrenalin level. You will keep going at peak efficiency whilst the task is still active. This euphoria stays with you through lunch. It is in the car, or on the motorbike, as you get five or six miles away that the let down occurs. Suddenly you feel tired. Your concentration can go entirely. You can be a danger to yourself and to others. Dramatic? Perhaps, but do be warned.

Coming home from a weekend a tutor was relaxing in the warmth of his colleague's car. The road was empty; it was Sunday afternoon. With no warning his colleague suddenly turned left, off the open road, and drove a complex pattern through side streets. Eventually he returned to the main road some four miles on having avoided a major junction that would have been jammed with traffic if it had been rush hour. He was totally unaware of his bizarre behaviour and a year later, when he was told about it at a party, he refused to believe the story.

WEEKEND OBJECTIVES

Underpinning your weekend will be objectives that were written in terms of your learning. It is upon these objectives that the weekend will be built.

181

Objectives for one NEBSM weekend were:

1. To help you prepare *effective* instruction.
2. To provide opportunities for you to practise effective instruction.
3. To increase your self-confidence.

These objectives cover the three basics of instruction — knowledge, skill, and attitude. For them to be achieved the weekend had to be structured to take the students through a course of instruction.

The level of success always has to be measured if a weekend is to be evaluated. In this case the evaluation criteria were written as:

Students: assessed and practical work throughout training module;
quality of response in end-of-year exam;
by observation of behaviour (by tutors) before, during and after the weekend;
by end-of-weekend evaluation.

Tutors: by self-assessment, followed by collective de-briefing;
by results of student evaluations.

Please note that the tutors evaluated their performance. It is only from such de-briefing that weekends can be improved year-on-year. (And tutor performance improved day-on-day.)

WHAT TO TAKE WITH YOU

Academic

Your class notes*,

textbooks*,

dictionary,

The Residential Weekend

pens — for writing on paper, for flip charts and for acetates,

pencil, eraser, ruler,

A4 lined pad, in ring binder,

calculator.

*As advised by your tutor.

Personal

Informal, but tidy, clothes. You will need clothes for the day, and to change into for the evening:

formal suit if required — your tutor will brief you,

spare pair of shoes,

underwear/linen/hosiery,

track suit/sports kit, if appropriate,

toiletries,

medication,

alka seltzer (or similar),

address book,

change for telephone,

cheque book and bank guarantee card,

radio,

towel if not going to an hotel.

WHAT TO LEAVE BEHIND

Leave the address and telephone number of the venue at home in case of urgent need.

183

STAYING AWAY

Most management weekends will be in good quality hotels, training centres or college halls of residence. When you arrive you will be asked to check in, that is to fill out a card with your name, address and details of the course. You will be told how to charge items to your account and you may be asked if you want a newspaper and/or a morning call.

You should know what is included in the course fee. It will normally not include anything except your room and meals. All extras are for you to settle first thing on the last day of the weekend. (It is best to do it before breakfast; when the desk is usually quiet.)

You should find a comfortable room, with everything that you need for a pleasant stay. If there is a problem do be reasonable but firm. You may have been asked to report any problem to the course tutor; if so, please do that as he or she has a continuing relationship with the hotel and will achieve more, quicker, than you will be able to.

Only use the telephone in your room if you want to pay the hotel's charges. There will be a public phone that will be far cheaper. (Why not get your home to ring you back in your room? That way you achieve privacy and yet avoid paying through the hotel.)

It is common for students to visit the bar before dinner, to drink with their meals, to have booze whilst in syndicate and to join with others in the bar at the end of each day. As an adult you will decide for yourself but too much alcohol will limit the value of the weekend. And you will feel and look awful on the last morning!

Meals are usually taken to time. Waiters commonly wait until a table is full before taking orders, so do be punctual. Sometimes you will find a choice of menu, but often a set meal will be provided. (This is partly because of budget, but more often to help the restaurant get you through quickly.)

If you have special dietary requirements you should have been asked by your tutor. If you haven't been it is usual for a restaurant to have a choice.

On one occasion that became famous a course tutor announced that vegetarians were catered for — instead of roast joint there was a choice of steak and kidney pie!

Coffee, or tea, is always available; but sometimes it is served in the lounge rather than the restaurant.

When relaxing in your room you may find a mini-bar. This will be stocked with a whole range of drinks. But they are expensive. They are not the hotel's gift to you!

You may also find that you can hire a video through your television. When browsing, be sure not to over-run your time unless you mean to watch, and to pay!

On the last morning of the weekend you will need to clear your room before you start work for the day. This may mean simply packing everything and leaving the case in your room. A special room may be available, or the back of the training room may be used. This allows the hotel to prepare your room for its next guest(s). Early access to the rooms will be part of the special price deal that will have been arranged with the hotel.

You will need to hand in your key to reception and to settle any account you have run up. Occasionally a student makes a mistake and orders something after his or her account is cleared. This only causes problems for the tutor, who has to sign for the whole weekend — and it catches up with the student very fast! Do try not to fall into this error.

MEETING THE ASSESSOR

The residential weekend is an excellent time for the assessor to meet you. And for you to meet the assessor. This can be a dreadfully formal and very stiff session where the assessor gets out in front and tells you all what a good course this is and how he or she is sure that you are benefiting.

This is a difficult session for everybody but it is very hard to avoid. How your assessor handles it will tell you a lot about what you should be doing to make a positive impact. Especially how you should present yourself when, and if, an oral interview is scheduled for the end of the course.

Assessors who fit with the timeplan, meet students informally, and build a relationship will learn far more about the course and everybody will be much happier. Your safeguard (if you need one) is that the assessor is not there not to judge you. He or she is there to assess the weekend and, in part, the course. He or she may use the time to go through assignments and personal journals with the course tutor, to discuss future assignments, perhaps to approve the final examination paper and marking scheme. It is such a good opportunity to get work done without the interruptions of daily life that much will take place of which you will not be aware. Of course it is nice for the assessor to get away to an hotel for lunch, or overnight, but the value far outweighs the cost.

ASSESSMENT

You need to determine whether any part of the weekend is part of the assessment procedure. Your course tutor will know and you should find out when you receive your briefing in the centre. If you are not told — ask! Do not assume. Ask!

Sometimes the whole of a weekend is assessed. (Not usually a weekend held early in the course.) Sometimes only one or two elements are assessed; academic opinion is divided over the value of assessment on a weekend. Some hold that assessment adds an edge to an exercise, that it motivates students. Others take the view that knowing one is under assessment causes some students to tighten up with

The Residential Weekend

nerves and that less learning takes place. Find out which view your course tutor holds. It is obviously important to you.

If there is to be assessment you need to know if it is individually or group based; what part of the weekend it affects; when it will be held; what are the criteria for success; who will carry out the assessment; what effect it will have upon the weekend; and what, if anything, it is necessary for you to know (or have with you) to maximise your chances of success.

SUMMARY

➤ Residential courses are exhilarating, but exhausting!

➤ Plan your personal learning objectives.

➤ Commit yourself to the weekend.

➤ Listen carefully to briefings.

➤ Check what, exactly, is needed on the weekend.

➤ Find out if any part of the weekend is assessed.

➤ Ensure that your family can contact you if needed.

➤ Arrive ahead of time and settle in.

➤ Check what is covered by the course fee and what you pay for yourself.

➤ Keep to time, especially meal times.

➤ Meet the assessor and make a positive impact.

➤ Check out early on the last day.

➤ Pay your bill!

FORWARD PLANNING IS THE KEY TO ENJOYMENT AND SUCCESS.

Section Four

The Examination

Formal examinations are taking less prominence in management courses. In many there are no formal examinations at all. So why include this section?

1. Some management courses still include examinations.

2. Many students will move on to take professional examinations, where the skills included in this section will be needed.

3. Assignments have grown larger and more significant, with the shift in emphasis away from end-of-course examinations.

4. In many ways some assignments resemble examinations, and you will be able to extract much valuable aid from this section.

Chapter 14
Preparing to Pass a Written Examination

Preparing to pass begins at the second you decide "I'm going to **pass**", not before.

Not at the moment you sign on for a course, not when the exam appears on your mental horizon — when you decide to pass.

Note: *Not when you hope to pass. Not if you expect to pass. Not if you think it would be a good idea to pass.* Only when **you decide** to *pass.*

At this stage of the book there are two classifications of reader. Those who have decided to pass and those who have yet to make the decision. First, a word to the undecided (the decided can read along too).

TO THE UNDECIDED

What benefit does a decision bring? It forces you to put your own pride up there on the line. Maybe not publicly, but it is better if it is public. Then you are letting yourself down if you don't get that pass. Declaring your intention to pass, putting yourself open to judgement from friends and relations is not easy, but it is essential. *You have to be committed.*

Of course you can always leave it to chance. They might invent brain transplants in time for your exam and you might be able to afford one.

They might ask very simple questions from an area of the syllabus you know something about. They might take pity on you.

Or you may feel that you already know so much about the subject that the exam is a formality. You may feel that your tutors are going to set things up so you can't fail. Do you? If so, do you know exactly how this exam is structured, what are the rules of this particular game? Are you skilled in exam technique? Subject knowledge and passing exams are not at all the same thing. Do you *really* believe that tutors who depend upon their professional integrity for a livelihood will set up a "milk run" for you?

Candidates in examinations make appalling errors! Not usually in subject knowledge but in exam technique. Appendix C shows what a range of examiners think. They are from the London Chamber of Commerce and Industry but the comments could have come from any examination, all candidates tend to make the same errors! And very few bother to learn examination technique.

You may feel that your tutor will get you through. He or she will, almost. Providing you are doing the work he or she recommends. Providing you keep disciplined you should have no trouble. But beware — a tutor cannot go into the exam room with you. A tutor can only go so far. Eventually you have to be self-sufficient. That's when an indecisive student crashes. Be warned.

CONTINUING FOR THE DECIDED

The longer ahead of the exam you decide to pass the greater the probability of success. Simply because, once *decided,* truly decided, you commit yourself to doing the work. If you are not working for an exam you are not committed — it is as simple as that.

With continuous assessment you are scheduled through your course.

Follow the schedule and your exam preparation times comes open just when you are ready. Unfortunately many students do not follow their schedule. They are late with assignments, in particular they are behind with their project. It all becomes a scramble. And the examination is what suffers. Or, to be accurate, the student suffers through not providing sufficient time for examination preparation.

A continuously assessed student has a tremendous advantage over one taking an externally set exam. He or she is working very closely with the tutors who set and mark the exam. Nobody is going to tell you the content of the paper, but it is fair and reasonable for tutors to indicate areas of the syllabus that should be given special attention. Equally you may be advised that certain areas are unlikely to come up this year.

Remember that the purpose is not to trick the student, nor is it to remove the challenge of the examination. A marking plan (or scheme) is determined at the same time as the exam questions are set. An assessor looks for a much higher level of achievement from students taking a continuously assessed paper when compared to the same students taking an exam set by an outside body.

EXAMINATION PREPARATION

Assuming that you have a month in which to seriously prepare for your examination, and assuming that like most students you have entirely forgotten what you were supposed to have learned six months ago, this is what you do:

1. Clear your social calendar for three evenings each week.

2. Secure a quiet area in which to work undisturbed. If necessary go to your centre library, or a library in a centre nearer to your home. (You don't usually have to be registered as a student at the second centre.)

3. Programme two hours and ten minutes into each evening. In

each session work 35 minutes on one subject. Then take 10 minutes out of your study area. In the open air if possible. (You need to blend academic and physical activity.)

Then 35 minutes on subject two, 15 minutes for coffee (no television).

Back for one more 35 minute session, and stop. Roll the subjects around day-by-day.

4. Ensure that your support team is on your side — your spouse, parents and close friends must know that it is only temporary but that it is definite. There can be *no* exceptions.

You have just over two hours blocked out three evenings a week for only a month — there is still time available for priority things (you can get out socially). And there are video recorders so you needn't miss important television.

For the organised student this regime probably slots into the places taken by the assignments and project anyway but don't forget the need to blend physical and mental activity. The temptation to stay too long with one topic *must* be avoided.

5. Get all the guidance you can from your tutor(s); but only believe it if you get it at first hand, or from your trusted buddy. Nobody means any harm but rumours abound at exam time.

6. Do look at past exam questions; probably they will be in the college library. But do check that the type and style of paper(s) has not been changed.

7. Determine you know which topics you are to concentrate upon. Then work them from the front, the side, upside down and inside out. You must know your topics thoroughly!

Plan answers to all the past questions you can get hold of.

Preparing to Pass a Written Examination

Refer back to textbooks after your first plan, then improve the plan. Refer back to your first plan as an aid to your second attempt to plan the question — then go back to the books to improve your plan. Always work from your mind and your notes first, textbooks only if needed.

If you can get a tutor to review your work — fine. It is worth asking. Don't assume that help is not available.

8. Reduce the topics to key points and get them first onto A4 sheets. Then reduce to A5. Finally put them on postcards. It is a good idea to have the question on the front and an outline of the answer on the back.

   Carry these cards everywhere and use them as flash cards (as self testers) when on the bus, the underground, waiting to see a client.

9. *Do not read a textbook.* Extract what you need but, for heaven's sake, don't read chunks of text. To pass you have to *understand*. To *understand* you have to *use*.

10. You are practising when you work on exam questions but you also need to practise under exam conditions. Plan, in your third week, to spend two full exam length evenings in a library. Set yourself up exactly as for an exam, with a past paper you haven't worked on before (seen, but not worked on). Work against the clock for two or three hours (however long your exam is). Put your papers away, *don't read them through* and pop off out to somewhere you can best relax.

    On the next evening be an examiner. Out of the pile of papers yours appears. Does it impress you? Is it well set out? Easy to read? Plenty of white space? Is the content satisfactory? Are the questions answered with the correct content *and* in the correct style? (If a report was called for have you written an essay?)

Has the correct number of questions been attempted? Is rough work shown; but at the back, out of the way?

Would *you* pass the candidate?

Again, there is opportunity to solicit the opinion of a tutor. Nothing ventured, nothing gained.

11. Check your exam answer plans against your flash cards. Go back to the book(s) at this stage only if absolutely necessary.

Keep your flash cards going up until the evening of two days before the exam.

You should do no exam work at all on the day before the exam. You will know it by then, or you won't. So remind yourself that the world is still there. Relax in your favourite way (don't overdo it!) Have a good night's sleep.

GENERAL COMMENT ON REVISION

Whatever you do *avoid* the standard form of "revision" used by almost all candidates. Do not sit for hours on end with the textbooks trying to cram knowledge into your head.

It is *not* knowledge of subject that is most important. You need *skill* in pulling out and presenting the right knowledge at the right time.

Skill comes only from practice. Revision has got to be active — you trying; failing; trying again, getting better; trying again, getting confident; trying again, getting it right; trying again, getting it perfected; trying again, getting it to a routine.

Pat Cash, the Australian tennis star, was being interviewed about his ability to win. "You can't win," he said, "until you have time to read the game and get to where the ball is going to be before it gets there. Then, if your shots are in the groove, you can pass the other player."

Preparing to Pass a Written Examination

Having time is what distinguishes the professional from the amateur. *You* have to become professional at passing examinations. That can only mean practice and rehearsal to get your skills "in the groove".

SUMMARY

➤ You have to *decide to pass* — nothing less will do.

➤ To pass you have to know the rules of your examination.

➤ You have to follow them too!

➤ A plan is essential; a plan in writing which you will follow.

➤ Clear your diary for the run in to the exam; schedule practice sessions and work up to exam speed.

➤ Get your support team on your side. Don't try to do it alone.

➤ Work from your notes, *not* from a textbook.

➤ Reduce your notes, gradually, to flash cards. Trust your mind.

➤ Work on the skills of communicating what you know.

➤ Examine your own work. Does it impress? Would you pass it?

➤ Work for the specific exam you are taking. (Exams are *not* all the same.)

➤ Do no exam work on the day before — if you don't know it by then an extra day won't help; and your brain needs a break.

EXAM PASSING IS A SKILL THAT YOU CAN LEARN.

Chapter 15
The Day of the Exam

The most important thing to control is panic. DON'T PANIC!

This is very easy to say, but very hard to do! Yet it is vital.

The best way to control your nerves is to understand what is happening to you. So, what is happening?

1. You are putting yourself at risk, in danger.

2. You are going into the unknown.

3. You are going into an atmosphere of stress and tension.

4. You badly want to do well, whatever you might say to friends to keep up appearances.

It will be the same for everyone else, one cannot avoid it — but *you* can control it if you understand what is happening, and why.

WHY DOES IT HAPPEN?

We possess very old-fashioned bodies and very old-fashioned mental systems. They were not designed for this century, nor have they adapted to it. So far as our autonomic (sub-conscious) systems are concerned, nerves are just a form of physical fear. There are only two responses to fear. One is to run away, the other is to stand and fight.

Both responses call for the same protective measures, which are completely automatic. The blood supply is taken back into the main body cavity, leaving just sufficient for function in the parts most at physical danger. The blood carrying vessels tighten down, to make them both smaller and tougher. A surge of adrenalin is automatically released. This substance (a hormone) is a very powerful stimulant. The whole body goes into a state of alert. Secondary systems like digestion are shut down; the body is ready to run, or to fight.

Unfortunately the exam candidate can do neither. There is a need for calm and for confident relaxation.

It is very important to recognise this and to take action to control the nervous energy that the body will provide for you. Start by thinking through the advantages of nervousness: you will be alert, perceptive, full of energy, ready to accept the challenge of the examination. Above all you will be in control of your destiny.

You, if you think about it, will form your own best solution to the problem of control over your own destiny.

THE BASIC RULES

1. Find out which room the exam will be held in. (Here you have a massive advantage over candidates taking external exams. They have to go to strange locations and cope with much that is unexpected.)

    Visit the exam room several days ahead. Walk around it, get the feel of it. Be sure *not* to decide where you want to sit! (This can be a great let down if you are told that you have to sit in another place on the day.)

    In everything you must have one aim — to know what is about

The Day of the Exam

to happen and to be prepared for as many eventualities as possible.

2. You may have to sit near a radiator, or in a cold room, so you will need to be able to vary your clothing. A shirt or blouse, with sweater and jacket gives you a range of options on the day. You have to be comfortable in yourself.

3. You know what you will need, but make a list well ahead of time and prepare two easy to carry bags at least 24 hours before the exam. (One can fit inside the other.) You will need to pack under two headings:

   (a) *What you need on the day* — basic day-to-day materials, packed lunch (can only go in on the morning), revision notes for the exam and perhaps for a second exam after lunch. This bag will have to be placed at the front of the exam room, out of your reach throughout the exam.

   (b) *What you need in the exam* — specialised materials, eg pens, pencils, rulers, calculator, etc; study notes and/or reference book(s) (if allowed), etc.

   You may be able to keep this bag with you on your desk or table, so you should also include some sweets, a small and carefully sealed drink or whatever is going to help you through the length of the exam. The guideline here is *not* to include anything that may upset other candidates (apples are noisy, oranges messy and smelly).

   If you need to add anything on the morning of the day, make a note of it the night before when you make your final check. In the morning you do not want to be harassed with detail, so get as much behind you as possible.

4. Be very careful about mascots. The good candidates' confidence can be shattered by simply forgetting a mascot!

201

5. The day starts early for most candidates; their nerves see to that! Fine, expect it. Be sure to have something to eat and drink, whatever your normal breakfast habit. An exam day is a different day so give your system something light to work on.

   Avoid any tranquilisers, anti-sick tablets, and so on. They may quell your tummy but they slow down your mental processes. Is it better to be sick? Probably, but if you have planned carefully you should be in charge of the situation and should not be so nervous as to need medical aid. (Don't say "But it always happens to me, I can't help it". You can help yourself to overcome the problem, if you think and plan ahead.)

   Often parents are the worst problem. They are so anxious that they screw you up with their nervousness. You should have dealt with this problem much earlier, by getting your support team on your side. If not, you must be prepared to cope with it now, probably by forcing yourself to be mature enough *not* to argue. It will do no good but instead set your adrenalin flowing in a negative, tightening and frustrating way.

6. Leave home in good time; you will know how long each part of the journey takes, so you should be able to be reasonably relaxed about the travel.

7. On the journey you will probably feel better if you go through your flash cards one last time. Or glance through your notes. But by now it is too late to affect your true knowledge. You are filling in your time and reinforcing the knowledge you already have.

8. At the end of the journey you should have some time in hand, so plan to use it well. *Don't* go into the centre and stand around with the other candidates. *Don't* stand around outside. Go to a coffee shop, or for a walk in the park.

   You must *not* become infected with the nerves of the other candidates. You cannot expect them to be as well prepared as you. They may not have read this book! There will be nervous ones, troubled ones, upset ones. The organised ones will be elsewhere, like you, securing their own peace of mind.

9. The exam room is not, to you, a centre room on the day. It is foreign territory. It belongs to the examiner and the invigilators. They allow you in and in a series of strict orders direct you where to sit, tell you to put your bags at the front of the room and not to touch the exam material until told.

   They treat you as naughty little children.

   This you have to counter. You are not a naughty child, so they cannot frighten you. In fact they can do nothing to you if you keep to the rules, nor do they want to. The invigilators are as much caught up in the exam game as the rest of us. They feel they have to behave as they do and we shan't be able to stop them. So, be prepared and with your carefully packed bags you can smoothly take possession of your desk.

10. *Take possession*—that is important. The space around you, your desk and chair should become yours, psychologically.

    The invigilators will have placed you, but you can still take charge. All you have to do is pick up the desk and move it, very slightly, to a different position. A position you have chosen. Move the chair too. Again, a very slight movement is all you need. But by taking charge you will exert a very strong psychological boost to your ego.

    It is a small technique, but a most valuable one. Remember you are playing a psychological game and you have to play to win.

11. *Do not write down formulae, etc* on exam stationery in the exam room before the exam starts. Any such notes, whilst reassuring to you (especially if you have fallen into the temptation to cram your very short-term memory in the minutes before the exam) leave you open to the charge of cheating. How could you prove that you didn't copy them in the room, or bring the notes in with

you? And you do not want an invigilator taking special notice of you at any stage. (Fill your time by carefully entering your name/number on every piece of exam stationery that is waiting for you.)

You also have to take charge of the exam paper, but that is for the next chapter.

SUMMARY

➤ It is natural to be nervous. Nerves can hinder or help.

➤ Nerves are *fear*. Fear of the unknown, fear of failure or of looking silly.

➤ The only person who should be frightened is the candidate who has done no proper preparation.

➤ Use nerves to your advantage. Channel them into heightened perception and an ability to concentrate and work for a longer stretch than is usual.

➤ Rehearse the day. Plan it ahead.

➤ Don't argue with parents, even if it means allowing them to fuss round you.

➤ Don't mix with ill-prepared candidates before the exam.

➤ Don't make short-term notes in the exam room in the minutes before the exam starts.

➤ Do take possession of your exam room space and equipment.

➤ Do very carefully enter your name/number on every piece of exam stationery.

➤ Do be entirely self-centred about the exam.

➤ Do give yourself every chance of passing.

PASSING IS THE PRODUCT OF PREPARATION.

Chapter 16
Your Examination Paper

You are sitting in the exam room. All is quiet now that candidates are settled. It is a horrid moment. Any time now the invigilators will bring round the exam paper. It can get very tense. Fine, this is not a problem. Why shouldn't you get tense? DON'T PANIC!

Then they make it worse by giving out the paper, face down, and you can't touch it. Then they look at the clock and wait for the second hand to sweep around. It's agony; can time ever move so slowly?

Be prepared for this anguish. Wait it out. It will all go in a rush when you can get to the paper, you just have to sweat through.

At last — "Turn the paper over, begin."

Here is where most candidates blow it completely. They rush; all their good intentions are forgotten in the excitement of the moment. It is a very powerful psychological release.

Again, *don't panic*. Breath deep, concentrate. Make that paper yours. Get on top of it. Pay no attention to anyone or anything else. Master the paper.

The style of examination paper can vary considerably. The tendency is away from the formal type: answer five questions from eight offered. Rather, you are likely to be asked to demonstrate your knowledge and skills in a more creative way. You will, of course, have had guidance on this from your course tutors.

Nevertheless, it is worth looking at a technique that works for a "five from eight" paper because it shows very clearly how it is possible to take charge. The technique works like this:

1. With a pencil in hand read down the questions very quickly. Don't try to analyse them, don't ponder over them.

2. Against each put either a tick, a cross, or a question mark. (A tick means you can do the question, a cross, "no way", a question mark, possibly.)

3. Count the ticks. If you have three or more you have a paper you can pass.

4. Count the question marks; if you have a further two you have a paper you can do well with.

5. Ignore *totally* the crosses. For you they *don't exist*. They are not a problem and must not get in your way.

So you are, very quickly, in a position to know how good a pass you can get.

If you have six ticks you have the happy task of choosing your best five questions. Any combination of two, three or four ticks plus three, two or one question marks focuses you onto your answers. But remember, you can pass with three tick questions. Here's how:

Each question = 20 marks. Pass = 50%

Ticked questions – you achieve 15 marks each. 3 x 15 = 45 marks.
Question marks – you achieve 8 each.   2 x 8 = 16 marks.

Total   = 61 marks.

Safety margin = 11 marks

Your Examination Paper

Even on "cross" questions, if you are forced to tackle one, you will pick up a mark or two. So the worst scenario could be:

Ticked questions	2 x 15 = 30
Question marks	2 x 8 = 16
Crosses	1 x 4 = 4
Total	= 50

But you should do better on question mark questions than 8 out of 20!

You work out the maths for yourself. Try a very good answer at 16, a medium at 12, a couple of fair answers at 9, a scrape at 4. Result? A pass!

You will know how your exam paper will be structured before you go into the exam. You should have worked out a method that works for you to remove the danger of panic setting in. And you will have practised. So you can reckon on being in possession of the facts about your likely result within a couple of minutes at most of the start of the exam.

The rest of the candidates will be sweating away. You won't have to, you will be taking a professional approach, and winning the game. But you still have to write your answers.

Now for a very hard thing for you to take on board. *Despite what everyone else will be doing* plan all your answers before you do anything else. You have to manage your time.

It is vital to plan answers, agreed? Then it is only a question of when to plan. You can take a three hour exam like this:

0 – 5 mins	Read paper — panic.
5 – 6 mins	Choose a question.
6 – 10 mins	Plan an answer.

Qualify in Management

10 – 40 mins	Write answer.
40 – 44 mins	Choose question and plan answer.
44 – 74 mins	Write answer.
74 – 80 mins	Choose question and plan answer.
80 – 110 mins	Write answer (trigger good fact that could have gone into first answer).
110 – 116 mins	Choose question and plan answer.
116 – 140 mins	Write answer (trigger other data that could have been used earlier).
140 – 145 mins	Choose question and plan answer.
145 – 180 mins	Write part of answer.

This is not a very effective use of time.

BEST SYSTEM FOR USE OF EXAM TIME

0 – 2 mins	Tick, cross, question mark.
2 – 6 mins	Select ticks and question marks.
6 – 30 mins	Plan answers to all questions, on one double spread of the answer book. Shift material around between questions so that it is used to best advantage. Include ideas for Q.1 generated whilst looking at Q.3. (How often does it happen? You are writing your third question, and an idea for your first is triggered.)
30 – 85 mins	Write the two answers that will most impress the examiner. (Good content, right style, well presented.)
85 – 90 mins	Break, stretch, relax, have a drink, look round, feel good.
90 – 170 mins	Write three answers.
170 – 180 mins	Read through, correct, check you name/number are on the answer book and on all sheets; and that extra sheets are tied into the book.

Your Examination Paper

You should feel pleased that others are scribbling away almost at once. The more who fail to plan properly, the more certain you are to get your pass!

To make even more certain you must ensure that your examiner is impressed with your paper. So tuck rough work away at the back. Don't put your rough work in the front of the book as it can have a minor negative effect no matter how experienced your examiner is.

Also note that the first three pages are crucial. Impression is everything at this point. You want the examiner to say "This is good, I wonder how good?", not "This is bad, I wonder how bad?"

Take your time to write neatly, space your work well and concentrate on saying the right things in a way that is calculated to impress.

Examinations for each course have a unique flavour. It is vital to understand precisely the form that your exam will take. You may be sitting an open book exam, where you have had briefing beforehand and are allowed to take notes and/or textbooks into the exam with you. You could be facing a multi-choice question paper. You may face a paper that mixes different styles of question. There is no way this can be predicted except by you finding out for yourself. Your course tutor will be glad to tell you. (In fact the last couple of weeks of the course will probably be nothing except exam preparation.)

Some guidance on question answering is in Chapter 18, but space is limited. Take advantage of the special offer (see page 275). The supplementary book contains examples of course material from actual management courses.

SUMMARY

▶ Take charge of the question paper. Use ticks, crosses and question marks to quickly select the questions you are going to answer.

▶ Do not worry about crossed questions, they do not apply to you and therefore they are not your problem.

▶ Plan your time. Maximise your marks by planning all answers at the beginning despite what the other candidates do.

▶ Make certain that the first three pages are impressive. You must catch the examiner's attention, early and positively.

▶ Plan a five minute break at about half way.

▶ Be sure to read through and catch as many errors as you can.

▶ Make certain you have named everything you are handing in and that all loose papers are tied into the main answer book.

PLAN AHEAD, PREPARE CAREFULLY, WORK FROM CONFIDENCE.

Chapter 17
Question Spotting

If anyone tells you that question spotting is unfair, don't believe them.

Your job is to use your skills and knowledge to pass an exam. You are required to study a series of subjects and to demonstrate a range of skills.

One important management skill is research. Question spotting is research, *applied research,* and quite legitimate.

"Question spotting" is not a precise enough term, however. What you should actually be doing is *topic spotting.* Three things are looked for by the examiner:

(a) subject knowledge;

(b) skill (ability) with the subject;

(c) skills of presentation.

Thus a question will call for a topic to be presented in a style that convinces the examiner that you have sufficient command of the knowledge; and an acceptable level of ability with it, to be allowed a pass, at least. Every effort to predict the topics that are most likely to be in your paper is worthwhile. It is also valuable to identify those with a low probability of inclusion.

You can seldom predict the style that the examiner will use on a particular topic. But you can often predict that a topic will be included.

Often, and with complete integrity, it is possible for a tutor to tell you exactly which topic(s) will be examined. (But not the actual questions.)

Even if you are not told the exact topics you should be able to work out with a fair degree of success which are most likely to come up and which are least likely to be included.

High probability

A major module on a topic that hasn't been tested by other means.

Lower probability

Topics which have been the subject of a major module. (Major assignment topics may be used as part of a question, or be needed in order to answer one fully. Statistics are a favourite here. They can be used across such a wide range of questions that, although they will probably have been in a major assignment, you must expect to be asked to apply a working knowledge of the subject.)

Low probability

A topic on the syllabus which has had little attention from the tutors.

Remember that you can always ask. Often you will be given guidance, if you ask for it.

Your theme must always be *pass*. A *pass* is what you want; a credit or a distinction would be nice. But to get a credit you first have to *pass*. Passing in the exam may only mean a need for 40%. Don't strive and struggle to no purpose. You will know roughly, perhaps exactly, what you need to do to achieve a pass overall. You will also know what you have to achieve to get better than a pass for the course overall. (It may be out of reach, given the marks you have achieved on assignments and the project.)

When preparing, you must allocate your efforts where they are needed, not to your favourite subjects; and *not* to the easy subjects only! It is the ones you find hardest that you need to motivate yourself to work upon.

EXTERNAL EXAMINATIONS

Here are two pieces of advice for when you have to take external examinations, perhaps for a professional institute. One is long, one is short.

1. It is best to use the same technique as the examiner and the moderator when attempting to calculate which topics will be in your paper. The examiner has to cover all topics in the syllabus, over a series of papers, and so has to have a tool to help with the planning.

    He or she must know what has been covered and when. Only then can the next paper be planned. A *matrix* is the best tool to use. They are easily made; you can make one for yourself when you need to.

    All you need is a large sheet of paper, perhaps A3, and question papers going back as far as is reasonable. Perhaps eight examinations over four years or five annual examinations. The example on the next page is an actual planning matrix produced by a college tutor for the Chartered Institute of Marketing's Fundamentals of Marketing paper. (Whatever examination you are to take the method is appropriate.)

    Study this matrix and decide which topics you would concentrate upon if you were going to take this exam. You don't have to be a marketing expert.

Qualify in Management

Institute of Marketing — Certificate
Fundamentals of Marketing

Requirement: Answer five from ten questions offered.

	1988 Nov	1988 June	1987 Nov	1987 June	1986 Nov	1986 June	1985 Nov	1985 June
Marketing concept	6	1/4	1	1	5	1	1	1
Marketing function	8		2/3	2	2		6	5
Marketing research	3	3	5	4	4	4	5	4
Pricing	4	6		7		7	8	8
Segmentation	1	2	4		6	6		7
Product planning	9	5	6	6			7	6
Sales force	5	7	9	8	8	8	9	9
Advertising	10	8	10	9	9			
Channels of distribution			8	3	3		3	3
Write notes on...			7	10	7	5	4	10
Communications mix						10		
Sales promotion							10	
Public relations		9						
Exhibitions						10		
Packaging						9		
Consumerism							2	2
Consumer behaviour	2							
Physical distribution						3		
Market structure						2		
Direct Marketing	7							
P.E.S.C.			10			1		
Organisation				5				

It is pretty obvious that marketing, marketing research and pricing are almost guaranteed to come up, isn't it? Closely followed in probability by segmentation and product planning.

Where a "Write notes on..." question is included it can be good for guaranteed marks since four topics are offered, with a maximum of five marks going to each. So an opportunity to answer a part question is offered; the examiner couldn't be doing more to help.

Obviously a concentration on the main topics that stand out is called for. From these alone a clear pass can be gained. An extra topic area will secure a comfortable pass.

If this sounds easy, it is because *it is easy,* given that you will take the time and trouble to analyse the task ahead of you and allocate your time and effort properly. *Note very carefully* that you still have to learn the topics thoroughly; you still have to understand the question so that you answer in the style required; and you still have to present your answer effectively.

That said, it remains true that time spent on a topic that is unlikely to come up is probably wasted. You do not have to cover the syllabus, you only have to answer the questions set.

Adopting this selection strategy has an element of risk — a topic you have ignored may come up. But, on the whole, it is a far lower risk than going in to an exam with a shallow knowledge across a wide range and no idea of what the examiner is likely to ask.

2. Buy the book from this series that specialises in your professional subject. Note its advice well, act upon it and pass.

SUMMARY

➤ Work out the probabilities of topics appearing.

➤ Predict the areas that *must* be questioned and the ones that are unlikely to be.

➤ Target your efforts so you are ready to answer in the selected topic areas.

➤ Don't worry about the other areas.

➤ Your focus must be on *passing* in each paper.

➤ You should know, roughly or exactly, the minimum you have to achieve.

NEVER BE AFRAID TO ASK YOUR TUTOR FOR GUIDANCE.

Chapter 18
Question Answering

What the examiners want and what they get are two different things and there is no excuse for this. Examiners' reports, year after year, say the same things. Generation after generation of students take no notice.

So why don't you be different? Why don't *you* do what the examiners want?

Appendix C contains extracts from a selection of examiners' reports from the London Chamber of Commerce and Industry's Commercial Education Scheme. Any set of examiners' reports is guaranteed to produce similar comments. The examples in this book have been taken from the LCCI because they have such a wide range of examinations. You should find it interesting that from 14 examiners across a wide range of subjects, covering students from a variety of ability levels, we have a consistent series of comments.

In summary they say:

➤ Prepare before the examination — subject *and* exam skills.

➤ Read and understand the question.

➤ Do as instructed in question.

➤ Answer the question set.

➤ Don't force knowledge into answers, *despite* the question set.

➤ Attempt an answer to the full number of questions.

➤ Allocate time and effort to marks available.

➤ Write answers that are long enough to cover the question.

➤ Show command of subject through practical examples.

➤ Read through and eliminate careless mistakes.

As the Selling and Sales Management examiner says: "Candidates should learn examination techniques".

You must also practise exam techniques. Note that almost all of the comments are about examination technique, not about subject knowledge. Be warned.

If so many candidates are ignoring the examiners' advice it must follow that an examiner is going to be so pleased to receive a script that is well presented and that answers the questions asked, that the natural inclination is to pass it. The only question is, "how good a pass to award"?

It is worth repeating that first impressions are vital. An examiner is likely to have a strong first impression. "This is a pass paper, how good?" Or "This is a fail paper, how bad?"

Good scripts are comparatively rare. Examiners are delighted to come across a really good script! So much so that the candidate who practises exam technique, especially presentation skills, must be pretty certain of a pass.

There is a very common fault that examiners come up against time and time again and make public in their reports. Hardly anybody listens.

The fault is to read a question to mean "Write everything I know about...".

Have you *ever* seen a question that says that? Nobody ever has and there is little chance anyone ever will! But candidate after candidate blasts off into answer after answer without any thought as to *what is actually asked*. If you do it you won't be alone, *but you will fail*.

Many examiners teach and they say that of the many, many classes they work with, up to and including post-graduate students, there is *always* the same problem. Students will *not* take time to read and understand the question!

An examiner, when teaching at a very large college south of London, always sets post-graduate students a piece of course work at the start of their second year. The wording changes, but the basic question is always: "Write a report, in 500 words, on the concept of marketing." For the first two years he set it without briefing and received (would you believe) essays, some of them extending to 5000 words!

In years three, four and five, he very carefully briefed students to read and understand the question. He also told them that, in the past, he had received 5000 word essays. Would you believe that he still receives long essays when asking for short reports!

And students (this is hard for him to accept) actually resent their long essays being returned. "I worked hard on that, it deserves marks" he is told.

Learn one vital lesson: **do what you are asked, or fail**.

If post-graduate students get it wrong on coursework, just think what a mess the more junior student makes. How fixed are you in your idea of what your examiners want. Where did your conception come from? There is some kind of folk myth handed on from generation to generation. Do not be taken in by it. The examiner's reports are clear and examiners are united across a range of subject areas.

Get your own examiners' reports, see what they say and learn from them. **Don't give the answer you want to, give the examiner the answer he or she wants.**

Remember, there are *three* things looked for:

➤ subject knowledge;

➤ skill (ability) with the subject;

➤ skills of presentation.

SUBJECT KNOWLEDGE

In Chapter 4 you learned that a student doesn't have to know everything about a subject. Can you remember the argument? (Look back if necessary and confirm it.) We also discussed this in Chapter 17.

SKILL WITH THE SUBJECT

You *must* be skilled within your subject. It is good learning practice to look at a subject from several viewpoints, so at one and the same time you can firmly establish some knowledge *and* practise examination technique.

An example will make the point clear: The examiner or teacher who asks for a 500 word answer on the marketing concept, as a first piece of course work, changes the wording from year to year. But only the wording changes. Look at these questions:

1. As part of the selection process for a post as marketing manager in industry write a 500 word report on the marketing concept.

2. You are newly appointed as marketing manager for a national

charity. Write a 500 word article on the marketing concept for inclusion in the staff magazine.

3. In 500 words show the managing director of a successful production oriented company why a marketing manager should be appointed.

Do you agree that these are different questions, but requiring the same basic knowledge?

These are *extremely* difficult questions to answer. (That's why they have been set to post-graduate students.) The limiting factor of 500 words means that students have to be very good at writing concise English. They also have to be good at analysing a situation and applying the marketing concept to it.

In each question they have to present the arguments for marketing to an audience with special perceptions and special needs. (The charity is not motivated by profit, the industrial firm certainly is. The magazine will want the material presented for a readership generally ignorant of marketing. The managing director will want to know why marketing is of value to his already successful firm.)

Also, in each case the student has a different role. In the first there is a need to get the job. In the second, to gain acceptance for marketing and for self. In the third, to provide a managing director with information that can be learned from and used as a basis for discussion with the board of directors.

Further, the style used must suit the requirements of the situation. The job application should include some personal marketing. The charity newsletter article should be chatty, interesting and informative. The managing director will want the information presented in a report written in crisp business English. The same basic knowledge is needed but used differently.

Thus, what you *must* do is get your mind around the basics of your subject and also practise using your knowledge in different ways. (For this you don't need pen and paper; you can do it as a mental exercise while on the top of a bus!)

SKILLS OF PRESENTATION

Presentation skills divide into *two* main areas:

(a) presentation of the content, logically and structured;

(b) physical presentation — neat, tidy, readable, impressive.

This subject is so important that the next chapter is devoted entirely to it.

How to discover what the examiner wants

There are *key words* that you must first look for in a question. (They are listed in Appendix D.) Key words are about *style:* they tell you what type of answer is needed. They are also about *content:* they tell you on what subject knowledge to focus the answer. So why look for *style words* first? Turn to the Appendix and check on "discuss", "outline" and "evaluate". Do you agree — each requires a different approach?

An examiner will give you a variety of questions to choose from. You can see that some will be easier in *style* for you; they will require less work. Always choose the ones with the minimum of work (provided you know the subject, of course).

Let us take three similar questions, using the key words you have checked.

Example 1

It has been said that general management is a skill that must be learned by any manager who intends to attain and secure a position on the board of directors. Discuss.

Example 2

Outline the skills of general management that are necessary for a director of a company to possess.

Example 3

Evaluate the general management skills that are needed if a company director is to be successful in his or her post.

Many candidates would focus on "general management" only. Some would write all they knew on the topic. Some would present an essay. Very few would write a report.

Some would write about "general management skills", again in a standard essay. Yet the examiner is asking the candidate to put his or her knowledge of general management into a context, to show three things:

1. *Knowledge* of management and of the skills a general manager needs.

2. *Skill* in using the correct style so that the set task is carried out. A discussion is very different from an evaluation; an outline is another requirement. An essay would be correct for the discussion answer, an essay or report for the evaluation, a report better for the outline.

3. *Presentation* of the knowledge, skilfully, so that it is comprehensible. (In other words the candidate's command of language, both in comprehension and use, is being tested.) This is a necessary skill for anyone who wishes to become a manager.

The examples show how the same knowledge could be tested in different ways. Obviously, the same topic will not appear three times on a paper. (If you think it has then you are misunderstanding the examiner.)

What is more likely to appear is a choice offering a range for the candidate to select from:

Q1. It has been said that general management is a skill that must be learned by any manager who intends to attain and secure a position on the board of directors. Discuss.

Q2. Outline the duties of the company secretary in a company.

Q3. Evaluate the benefits of a management training scheme for new recruits of high potential in an international company.

These would test the same skills of comprehension and presentation, whilst offering a range of topic areas from which to choose. Thus you must be able to answer a topic in a range of styles. *There is little point giving an examiner a brilliant essay if he or she is asking for a short report.*

If you were offered these choices you should immediately evaluate your chances of success, using the tick, cross, question mark technique. Your logic will be unique to you, but a typical logic *could* be:

▶ Discount Q1 immediately — "discuss" questions can be open-ended and they certainly require an extensive answer that is well presented. They look easy on first reading, but they can be beasts to answer well. Cross it.

▶ Outline. Great! Do I know about the subject? Enough? Tick it.

▶ Evaluate, a very practical job, if I know about the subject. Do I? Put a question mark.

Only if you can't find five ticks and/or question marks from the eight questions do you go back to choose from the crossed questions. Use these as your last answer(s), plan very carefully to pick up every mark you can and don't try to pretend that you would have been able to answer fully if you hadn't run out of time.

This *very old* trick of pretending to run out of time is based on the hope that the examiner will say "What a shame because the candidate did know the subject, I'll add a couple of marks because they are deserved". Actually what happens is that the examiner either thinks "Not this old trick again" or "Candidates are supposed to manage their time, this one hasn't. I'm not at all impressed by that". Either way no benefit is gained by the candidate.

The examiner can only mark what is in the candidate's paper. If time is a problem, and it can be, it is better to answer the final question in note form. You then give then examiner an opportunity to give marks for knowledge, and something for style.

A last point: in Question 2 many candidates would write well about the duties of a secretary (ie a shorthand typist or assistant) rather than a secretary of a company. Their perceptive skills would let them down. In their panic the key word they would see would be "secretary".

You must look for style and for content; style first, content second.

SUMMARY

➤ Examiners, who *know*, say what they want.

➤ Students are not giving it to them.

➤ Students are failing.

➤ Examiners are not happy, students are unhappy.

➤ Examiners are not going to change.

➤ The student who wants to pass must play the examiners' game — the rules are clear.

➤ Many students won't know the rules and won't bother to find out.

➤ Many students will *fail*.

➤ You do not have to be one of them.

GIVE THE EXAMINER WHAT IS CALLED FOR.

Chapter 19
Presenting Your Work

It is crucially important to present your work in the form that is required. Whether you are working on an assignment or an examination question you have the same basic task: to carefully analyse the assignment or question, carefully plan your answer, present it impressively. The physical presentation of work is tremendously important, the more so in a management course.

Read the term "examiner" throughout this chapter to include tutors, assessors, moderators, employers, anyone to whom you are presenting work.

Consider the need to *impress* the examiner. If you were an examiner you would receive about 400 exam papers in a large parcel. You are going to have to read up to 400 versions of answers to the same questions! Immediately there has got to be a boredom problem. An "I've seen this answer so many times before" problem.

Your problem is to get the examiner to take special notice of *your* paper. You really do want to impress the examiner. You should be aiming for an immediate (and unconscious) reaction — "Hello, here's one who knows what he or she is talking about". (Remember perception — get the examiner's senses, including his or her sixth sense, working for you.)

You have got to present your paper in such a way that the examiner feels, immediately, that you should pass. Achieve this and you are 10% of the way to a pass. It is incredibly important.

A shorter answer that directly responds to the examiner's need and which is presented in a clear style will impress and attract high marks.

As has been explained earlier in this book there is need to look for *key words:* key words for content required and key words for style. Once this has been done you must select which question(s) to answer, if you have a choice!

Then you must choose how to present your answer. Your content must be perceived how you intend, and the appearance of your work must add to its value.

CONTENT PRESENTATION

There is need to structure your work so that your reader (or listener) is taken through your answer in a logical way that makes sense to them and which they understand. Let us take these three key factors one by one.

Take your reader (or listener) through in a logical way

Point must follow point, with each developing your case. Each of your points should flow from the preceding one. When planning your answer you will find yourself roughing out paragraph eight and discover that something should have been said earlier. It is needed earlier, to help you now. Find this out in the planning stage. The prime purpose of answer planning is to eliminate this problem. Examiners know instantly which students have taken time to plan and which have blasted straight into their answers without careful forethought.

There is an old cliche — "failing to plan is planning to fail". Old it may be, cliche it certainly is. But *failing to plan* is a key reason for so many poor pieces of work. Always take 10% of the time available to plan your work.

Presenting Your Work

That makes sense to them

To them! They, your reader(s) or listener(s) must find your work sensible. If they don't you will have wasted your time. It follows that you must write, or speak, with the needs of your audience in mind. Obviously you must say what is correct, but say it in a way that will appear sensible to your audience.

What is "sensible" is a matter of judgement. And judgement is usually subjective. Look up "sensible" in a dictionary. The Concise Oxford defines it in four ways; the one that is applicable here is "Having or showing good sense, reasonable, judicious, moderate, practical (*a sensible man.. that is very sensible of him)*".

What will your audience find sensible? What examples should you use? How will their built in perceptions and biases affect their judgement of your work?

A student on a management course, asked to draft notes for a talk to a Women's Institute meeting, took as his examples two of the British Government's current advertising campaigns. One was for the privatisation of a public utility, the other a campaign about AIDS. Both are highly charged topics. The first was a political hotbed, where the audience were bound to have their own pre-conceptions. The second discussed birth control methods in language that the audience had been brought up, as gentlewomen, to regard as highly personal and extremely private. He was judged not to have been very sensible in his choice of examples. His heated response that "They ought to know about such things and they ought to be able to be dispassionate about them" only underlined a terrible lack of awareness of the sensibilities of others. Not a trait one looks for in a manager.

Which they understand

The need to understand comes up time and again doesn't it? It can only be because it is of key importance.

Your audience must understand you. Your logic must match theirs;

231

or they must be taken very carefully through the process of your logic. You must take them from point to point, not moving on until each point is fully covered, so that you keep them with you.

All tutors have made this mistake; one works away with a group of students and develops a concept over perhaps half a day. All is going well, the group seems very happy, the tutor is looking forward to a well earned lunch. In closing the morning the killing questions are asked "Does everyone understand?". "Is there any point I should go over?" One student puts up his hand. "Please — that point about..." It is a key point, one that was covered two hours ago, one that supported the entire structure of the morning! The tutor failed to communicate. Someone didn't understand, and the tutor didn't notice. It happens to all tutors but it happens very seldom to the tutors who plan thoroughly and who check understanding as they progress.

It is *never* acceptable to write all you know about a subject.

It is *essential* that you give just enough knowledge, demonstrate the required skills and use the correct style. A short answer that does this will always beat a rambling un-structured response.

Whilst this section was being drafted (whilst it was actually up on the screen of the word processor) an envelope came through the front door. It contained an assignment that a management student had been set as a major piece of course work. Let us call the student Z.

Z's tutor was unhappy with the work and thought it worth 17% at most. It went to the course director for a second opinion and from there to the head of department. Nobody was satisfied with the work, but to be absolutely certain the advice of an independent experienced examiner was asked.

The assignment is dreadful! It is submitted by a mature student with a high level of intelligence, towards the end of a senior management course. It is ten pages long (about 2000 words) and there are over 100 errors of basic grammar and presentation!

First impressions:

(a) The student's name is an unreadable signature!
(b) Underlining is freehand and crooked.
(c) Words, phrases, even one *sentence,* are deleted by scribble.
(d) Careless spelling errors have not been noticed.
(e) The work is a bunch of A4 sheets. They are not clipped together and no attempt has been made to present them professionally.

So, before one can examine the content of the assignment one has to break through the obstacles that the student has erected.

Content:

1. There were four questions to answer. A report to senior management was specified. Z has written an essay. An essay that rambles.

2. Z consistently uses Guinness as an example, extolling the success of Guinness with stout. Yet the stout market is declining, has been for years, and Guinness has tried everything to reverse the decline, without success. Entirely the wrong example to choose.

3. Z's fourth paragraph reads "Given the weak position of XYZ Company vis-a-vis the other major competitor — both in market share and public house outlets , and also in terms of off-sales outlets that XYZ is weak".

    No, it doesn't make sense. Yet it is handed in as part of a major assignment. Z cannot have read through the work.

4. The questions have not been answered, the underlying theory has been discussed superficially and no management report has been written.

There were many more errors, but these are surely sufficient to illustrate the extremely low quality of the work!

Overall comment now attached to the assignment:

This is totally unacceptable as a submission. Even basic errors are committed — including errors of syntax; basic presentation skills are ignored. Appendices are attached, but most not referred to. Those that are used are not appropriate to their given purpose.

Management knowledge is sketchy and highly generalised. Examiner's instructions are ignored. This should be a report upon which management action could be taken. It is, instead, a rambling document that shows a lack of concern for the reader and demonstrates the writer's inability with both subject and presentation skills.

You may well ask why work that is dreadful has been passed through so many tutors for comment. This is a good question. The answer lies in the in-built desire of the tutors to be scrupulously fair with students. The tutor who set the assignment is younger and less worldly than the student. The course tutor is not subject skilled in this assignment's topic, nor is the head of department. Everybody wants student Z to pass, but this assignment has to be re-submitted and Z has to accept that. Therefore, a body of informed opinion needs to be assembled to convince Z. It is very time consuming and apparently wasteful of resources, but it is evidence of the care with which a good centre monitors the work of both its students and its tutors.

PHYSICAL PRESENTATION

The examiner must be impressed by your paper. The first response is critical. It is likely to be "This is good, how good?" or "This is bad, how bad?" Student Z's work actually offends. That a student can be so arrogant as to submit work of such an inferior standard is insulting to the reader. One cannot avoid an immediate perceptual judgement and good presentation is the key to this.

An examiner understands if a student has difficulty with a subject but will not tolerate a management student who doesn't take the trouble to present work to a high standard. The actual layout, crispness and overall impression are powerful influencers for good, or ill.

The basic rules are:

1. Make your work easy to read, and easy to understand.
2. Write short sentences. (8-14 words.)
3. Use short paragraphs. (3-5 sentences.)
4. One subject per sentence. One topic per paragraph.
5. **Never** use a long word when a short one can replace it.
6. Use specialised language only when writing to fellow specialists.
7. Avoid (or at least explain) specialised language only when in doubt about your reader's understanding.
8. Use initials only *after* using the full title. (eg The Royal Automobile Club of Great Britain (RAC) has close associations with motor sport. The RAC has its head office in Pall Mall, London.)
9. Space your work on the page. Don't cramp it. Never use narrow-lined paper. Leave generous margins.
10. Leave a half page between answers, or between sections of an answer.
11. Read through your work and neatly correct any errors.
12. Present your work in a folder or a binder that personalises it.
13. Name and date your work. On the front. At the top.
14. Keep a copy.

Always do what the examiner requires.

Answer the question(s).

In a formal examination add these rules to those above:

1. Write your name and/or number clearly and neatly on the front of the answer book. Tick the questions you have answered, if you are asked to do so.
2. Do all your rough work in the *back* of the answer book. (No matter how professional the examiner it is better for him or her not to see rough work before anything else.)
3. Start your first answer on the right hand page.
4. Never use a red or green pen. (These are the examiner's colours.)
5. Write your second best answer first. This allows you to relax into the paper, yet presents a good impression to the examiner.
6. Make your first three pages especially crisp, clean and neat.

PERSONAL PRESENTATIONS

Often you will be required to make an oral presentation. Usually you will also be required to submit a written report.

One important tip is that written English is very different from spoken English. Use your report as the foundation of your presentation but do not read from it. Reading a script is possible, to the skilled, if the script is written in spoken English. Very few people can write spoken English, so don't try.

Take the two tasks as similar but separate. Research and write your report in written English. Clear your mind of the structure and of the syntax.

Take your report *as though it were written by somebody else* and translate it into spoken English. Use 6" x 4" cards and put header notes on each. Then speak naturally from the notes. Rehearse your presentation.

Your knowledge of the report will be fed to you by your sub-conscious. You will be able to concentrate upon the audience, and adjust your words to fit their need. Your presentation will be relaxed. The series of hooks and triggers that you set up in your notes, plus the confidence that comes from practice, will ensure that. Those who read their reports will come over as stilted and uncomfortable. And they won't be able to look at their audience to measure the levels of understanding and interest.

SUMMARY

- Passing assessments and examinations is easier than most people think.
- Analyse the requirement, plan the answer, present it impressively.
- Key words clearly identify the examiner's requirements.
- Length is *not* needed, nor is volume. Quality is.
- Content must be presented in logical structure.
- Work to establish understanding.
- Never write all you know about a subject.
- Keep a copy of your work.
- Always do what the examiner requires.
- Use your time to the best advantage.
- Put rough work in the back of an exam answering book.
- Name and/or number your work, every page in an exam script.
- Written and spoken English are different.
- Watch your audience, judge their level of understanding and interest.
- Trust your sub-conscious and the hooks and triggers you have established.

FAILING TO PLAN IS PLANNING TO FAIL.

Chapter 20
The Oral Interview

The "oral interview" may be its title, but for the student it is an examination. It shouldn't be and it is not meant to be, but when one is being assessed it is natural to feel that one is being examined. We shall use the word "interview" rather than "examination" in this chapter, but not lose sight of the examination-type stress that you are likely to feel.

The oral interview can be made into an ordeal, if you want it to be one. It is never going to be tremendously enjoyable because the experience is new to you (or one that you meet seldom) and you will have some degree of nervousness about it.

Think of it as similar, but much less pressured, than a job interview. Less pressured because you are not competing with others for work. Everyone can and should pass their oral interview.

WHY HAVE ORAL INTERVIEWS?

1. To allow the assessor direct contact with every individual student.
2. To confirm that each student can communicate effectively.
3. To allow any compensated passes to be verified.

It is very important that managers are able to communicate effectively. Management is the achievement of results through people. Your ability to communicate in writing will have been tested throughout the course. You will have made oral presentations and probably carried through some training sessions. The last thing left to check is oral effectiveness on a one-to-one, or one-to-two basis.

Usually this is not a marked element of the course. It is confirmation because it is almost unknown for a student to fail at this stage. Remember that — it is almost unknown for a student to fail at this stage.

The interview will usually be between you as an individual and the assessor. The course tutor may be present but in a supporting role only. Concentrate upon the assessor; the purpose of the meeting is for him or her to confirm that you are management material.

INTERVIEW OBJECTIVES

An interview has been defined as *a conversation with an objective*. You have to determine what are your objectives. Your list will probably look something like the following:

1. To impress the assessor with my management qualities.
2. To amplify and/or explain my work on the course.
3. To discuss aspects of the course.
4. To enjoy the experience.
5. To pass.

The assessor has to have something on which to base the interview. What can he or she take?

1. Your project.
2. An excellent piece of your course work.
3. A weak piece of your course work.

4. The residential weekend.
5. The course overall.
6. The response of your employer.
7. Perhaps something personal which you will know about.

Go into the interview with the knowledge that the assessor wants to pass you. (He or she is in education to pass people and it is much easier to pass, as we have discussed earlier in the book.)

You are aiming to get into conversation, not simply respond to questions.

PREPARATION

Do not be complacent. Take the experience seriously. Prepare yourself. Look through your course work and note anything you are especially proud of or which was extremely hard to complete. Refresh yourself on your project. Prepare to introduce some areas into the conversation so that it is not entirely questions from the assessor and answers from you.

You will have met the assessor and, hopefully, made a good impression. You will be well placed to pick up on that. What did you talk about before? What are his or her special interests (or fads). What will he or she respond to favourably and what negatively?

How have your employers responded to you taking the course? How has your direct boss responded? This is an area that is almost bound to come up and you can always raise it yourself. Educationalists are very interested in the reactions of employers who sponsor students.

Dress appropriately. You are being interviewed as a manager. Dress how a manager dresses in your business: clean hair and clean shoes. Aim to give the impression that you normally look as you do for the interview, that you haven't dressed up for the occasion. (You will have dressed up, of course. But you don't want to give that impression.)

Arrive in good time for the interview. Check in as instructed. Confirm in a mirror that your appearance is all it should be. (Females tend to do this automatically, males are much more careless!) Keep your nerves under control in whichever way is best for you. Don't spill coffee over yourself at this late moment!

THE INTERVIEW

Probably it will not last more than ten minutes — the assessor has to see all the students and time will be short.

Are you being interviewed early in the session or late? This makes a big difference to the way you should handle yourself. If you have an interview early in the day the assessor will be fresh and will not have current information on the course. He or she will be less able to respond to your views on the course.

The assessor will be probing for new information from which a dossier will unconsciously build up. Later in the day the questions are likely to be much more informed and he or she will be able to enter into a discussion about the course using information obtained from your fellow students.

Depending on how organised the assessor is, you may find the ten minutes running over. Timekeeping will be much tighter later in the day and you may not get your full 10 minutes. The assessor will be tired, and perhaps a little jaded. It will be your job to feed material that rejuvenates.

Whatever time of day it is, always enter with a smile and a firm handshake. Speak to the assessor by name: "Good morning Mr Jones". If your assessor is "old school" the tradition of formality up and informality down may apply. (You use Mr (or Mrs), he or she calls you by your first name.) If your assessor is used to this style it will do you no harm to accommodate him or her. If your course tutor is known by his or her first name then it is probably alright to use it in the interview. But avoid the problem if you can. It will not be wrong to use Mr or Mrs to or about the tutor. (It would be too formal to use Sir or Madam in this context unless it comes naturally to you.)

You *must* sit upright (no slouching) and look alert. Aim for a 60:40 split of conversation, with you contributing 60%.

When the interview is over, say "goodbye and thank you" in the manner that is most appropriate. Again, use the assessor's name.

Avoid asking questions like "When will I hear the result?" Your course tutor can tell you routine things like that outside the interview room.

If you are a marginal student

You will know how well you have done on the course and you will know what your aggregated results are. If you have a compensated pass, or if you are hoping to obtain one, then the importance of the interview changes dramatically.

You will still need a set of objectives. One will be to convince the assessor that you deserve a compensated pass. (Everybody will want you to have a pass but you have to provide the evidence to allow it to be granted.)

You will know where the problem is. Often it is in a numerical subject but sometimes very good supervisors are not skilled at writing management quality reports. You have to show that you:

(a) have worked very hard to master the topic;

(b) are determined to succeed;

(c) are making definite progress;

(d) are committed to making a success of management;

(e) are a capable manager in practical terms.

Qualify in Management

You may be asked to talk the assessor through an assignment that you found difficulty in writing. (The concern is that you *know* the subject even if you have difficulty communicating it.)

You may be asked to explain why a certain numerical technique is used and where you would turn to for help. A manager obtains results through people, so it is perfectly acceptable to know what a technique will do for you but not be able to calculate the numbers for yourself. In this case you need to show that you have sufficient confidence to call for what you need from a specialist and sufficient understanding to be able to use the data when it is ready.

Management is about confidence and leadership:

A newcomer to sailing went out in a dinghy with a friend who was a very experienced sailor. Bad weather blew up, the boat was thrown about wildly and things looked bad. The novice looked up from the bottom of the boat, where he had been put to bail the water out, and was reassured to see his friend comfortably lodged into the stern of the dinghy without a care in the world. Eventually they reached the beach, de-rigged the boat and went into the clubhouse.
"For a time I thought we were not going to get back" said the novice.
"So did I!" his friend replied.

SUMMARY

▶ Oral interviews are not really examinations, except to you!

▶ They exist to confirm management ability and, sometimes, to confirm a compensated pass.

▶ Prepare for them carefully:
set clear objectives;
review course work, journal and project;
dress appropriately — clean shoes, clean hair.

▶ Arrive in good time.

▶ Greet the assessor by name.

▶ Smile.

PASS THROUGH CLARITY OF PURPOSE, COUPLED WITH SELF-CONTROL.

Section Five

The Key Points

Chapter 21
Conclusion

A summary of the Chapter Summaries

Passing management courses is not difficult, given the right preparation.
Self-analyse — *you* have to pass. *You* have to *want* to pass.
Match incentive to motivation.
Be responsible for your own learning.
Get your support team on your side — involve your family.

Set up your notes with hooks and triggers.
Use recall/review/recognition techniques.
Knowledge, skill and attitude are all important.
Understand and use — the Double U principle.

Learning is memory *plus* understanding.
Work from your notes — not from textbooks.
Mix academic and physical activity; minimise stress.
Target your efforts.
Expect learning plateaux and plan for them.
SQ3R — Survey, Question, Read, Recall, Review.

Discover your course structure.
Identify the assessment scheme.

Maintain a course diary.
Set up a buddy system.
Assume help is available — and use it.
Use textbooks as tools.

Manage your time.
Enjoy your course; commit yourself to it.
Share your knowledge and skills.
Beware the time, tutor and tangent traps.
Provide exactly what each assignment requires.
Submit to a person, note who and when.
Hit your deadlines.
Keep a copy of your work.

Everybody wants you to pass.
Answer the questions asked — in the style required.
Plan a positive presentation — DON'T PANIC.

Rehearse the day of the exam.
Plan your time.
Expect to be nervous — use the energy positively.
Take possession of your part of the exam room.

Write your name/number on all exam stationery.

Tick, cross and questionmark to select your questions.
Quality, not length will get you through.
Share your knowledge around the answers.
If in doubt — use report style.
Always quantify where you can.
Read through and polish your answers.
Get to know your moderator.
Impress, simplify.
Smile.

Conclusion

SUMMARY

➤ Be responsible for your own learning.

➤ Understand and use — the Double U principle.

➤ Mix academic and physical activity — minimise stress.

➤ Target your efforts.

➤ Manage your time.

➤ Set up a buddy system.

➤ Discover your course structure.

➤ Provide the *exact* requirements of each assignment.

➤ Share your knowledge and skills.

➤ Submit to time.

➤ Keep a copy of your work.

➤ Answer the questions asked — in the style required.

➤ Expect to be nervous at times — use the energy positively.

➤ Write your name/number on all exam stationary.

➤ Quality, not length will get you through.

➤ Share your knowledge around the answers.

➤ If in doubt — use report style.

Qualify in Management

- ➤ Always quantify where you can.
- ➤ Get to know your moderator.
- ➤ Focus on *passing*.
- ➤ Plan and practice.
- ➤ DON'T PANIC.

PASS

Appendix A
Recommended Reading

Study Techniques: Hints for Students	Bjernum	Harrap
Use Your Head	Buzan	BBC
Lateral Thinking	de Bono	Pelican
Study for Success	Courtney	Intertext
Study to Succeed	Hills	Pan
A Student's Guide to Efficient Study	James	Pergamon
A Student's Guide to Study	Laugharne	Intertext
How to Study	Maddox	Pan
Study Faster and Retain More	MacGibbon & Kee	Reading Laboratory
Effective Study	Robinson	Harper & Row
Accelerated Learning	Rose	Accelerated Learning Systems Ltd

Appendix B
Moderator's Report Form

Validating bodies very strictly control the quality of their courses. They are extremely thorough in their monitoring of quality and set out their requirements in considerable detail.

Moderators are required to report on every facet of each course, with the prime intention of helping the course team to set and maintain the highest standards.

Each validating body has its own methodology, that adopted by BTEC is a good example. You will see that a Moderator's task is far from easy.

The Moderator's Report Form is reproduced by kind permission of BTEC.

Qualify in Management

Page 1
[rev 8/89]

Business & Technician Education Council **BTEC**

For BTEC's use

Moderator Report Form

Visit date	17 – 22
Visit type	A/23
Duration (hours)	A/26 – 27
Report type	A/28

To ensure that all copies are clear, please type or complete in ball-point pen

1 Moderator, centre and visit details

Moderator's name _____ Moderator no _____ 5 – 10

Centre name _____ Centre no _____ 11 – 16

Course/qualification title and main study area (if applicable)	Course No(s)	Level	Course mode(s) of study	Number of students in:			
				1st year	2nd year	3rd year	
							B/27 – 43
							B/44 – 60
							B/61 – 77
							B/78 – 94
							B/95 – 111

Main purpose of visit

Key people met (and their position)

2 Action plans

Please circle

Have the priorities for action identified at the last visit been carried out in respect of: yes no n/a

2.1 course management and team operation	1	2	X	C/26
2.2 teaching and learning strategies	1	2	X	C/27
2.3 assessment strategy	1	2	X	C/28
2.4 course review and evaluation	1	2	X	C/29
2.5 equality of opportunity (opportunities for study are open and equal so that there is no hazard to fairness in relation to gender, race or religion)	1	2	X	C/30
2.6 implementation of the requirements of the approval (where a course has been newly approved or reapproved, have the requirements of the approval been implemented?)	1	2	X	C/31

3 Priorities for action before next visit

3.1 By the centre

Action form from Regional Coordinator received

3.2 By the moderator

Action taken

Date of next visit

Moderator's signature _____ Date _____

M063/1

Appendices

Page 2
(rev 8/89)

Moderator no
Centre no
Visit date

For BTEC's use

4 Please describe aspects of good practice noted during visit

Tick if Section 4 completed ☐   C/32

5 Course management and team operation

Key Issues	Level	Low Ratings (please circle) High	Not covered	
5.1 Course team's liaison with moderator	F	1 2 3 4 5 6	X	D/26
	N	1 2 3 4 5 6	X	D/27
	H	1 2 3 4 5 6	X	D/28
	CE	1 2 3 4 5 6	X	D/29
5.2 Recruitment, induction and progression policy	F	1 2 3 4 5 6	X	D/30
	N	1 2 3 4 5 6	X	D/31
	H	1 2 3 4 5 6	X	D/32
	CE	1 2 3 4 5 6	X	D/33
5.3 System for course monitoring	F	1 2 3 4 5 6	X	D/34
	N	1 2 3 4 5 6	X	D/35
	H	1 2 3 4 5 6	X	D/36
	CE	1 2 3 4 5 6	X	D/37
5.4 Strategy for course delivery	F	1 2 3 4 5 6	X	D/38
	N	1 2 3 4 5 6	X	D/39
	H	1 2 3 4 5 6	X	D/40
	CE	1 2 3 4 5 6	X	D/41
5.5 Quality of employer links (see also 6.3, 7.4 and 8.2)	F	1 2 3 4 5 6	X	D/42
	N	1 2 3 4 5 6	X	D/43
	H	1 2 3 4 5 6	X	D/44
	CE	1 2 3 4 5 6	X	D/45
5.6 Planning, deployment, management of resources	F	1 2 3 4 5 6	X	D/46
	N	1 2 3 4 5 6	X	D/47
	H	1 2 3 4 5 6	X	D/48
	CE	1 2 3 4 5 6	X	D/49

Please tick this box if Section 5 **not** covered during visit ☐   D/50

M063/2

Qualify in Management

Page 3
[rev 8/89]

Moderator no

Centre no

Visit date

For BTEC's use

6 Teaching and learning strategies

Key Issues	Level	Low	Ratings (please circle)	High	Not covered	
6.1 Use of student-centred practical learning activites	F	1 2 3 4 5 6	X	E/26
	N	1 2 3 4 5 6	X	E/27
	H	1 2 3 4 5 6	X	E/28
	CE	1 2 3 4 5 6	X	E/29
6.2 Use of core themes for integration within and between units	F	1 2 3 4 5 6	X	E/30
	N	1 2 3 4 5 6	X	E/31
	H	1 2 3 4 5 6	X	E/32
	CE	1 2 3 4 5 6	X	E/33
6.3 Practical work and assignments are realistic and work-related	F	1 2 3 4 5 6	X	E/34
	N	1 2 3 4 5 6	X	E/35
	H	1 2 3 4 5 6	X	E/36
	CE	1 2 3 4 5 6	X	E/37
6.4 Recognisable and coherent programme of integrative assignments	F	1 2 3 4 5 6	X	E/38
	N	1 2 3 4 5 6	X	E/39
	H	1 2 3 4 5 6	X	E/40
6.5 Positive development of common skills	F	1 2 3 4 5 6	X	E/42
	N	1 2 3 4 5 6	X	E/43
	H	1 2 3 4 5 6	X	E/44
6.6 Design of work experience for full-time students	F	1 2 3 4 5 6	X	E/46
	N	1 2 3 4 5 6	X	E/47
	H	1 2 3 4 5 6	X	E/48
	CE	1 2 3 4 5 6	X	E/49
6.7 Students' response to course	F	1 2 3 4 5 6	X	E/50
	N	1 2 3 4 5 6	X	E/51
	H	1 2 3 4 5 6	X	E/52
	CE	1 2 3 4 5 6	X	E/53

Please tick this box if Section 6 **not** covered during visit ☐   E/54

M063/3

Appendices

Page 4
[rev 8/89]

Moderator no
Centre no
Visit date

For BTEC's use

7 Assessment strategy

Key Issues	Level	Low Ratings (please circle) High	Not covered	
7.1 Validity of assessment	F	1 2 3 4 5 6	X	F/26
	N	1 2 3 4 5 6	X	F/27
	H	1 2 3 4 5 6	X	F/28
	CE	1 2 3 4 5 6	X	F/29
7.2 Balance of assessment methods	F	1 2 3 4 5 6	X	F/30
	N	1 2 3 4 5 6	X	F/31
	H	1 2 3 4 5 6	X	F/32
	CE	1 2 3 4 5 6	X	F/33
7.3 Assessment criteria	F	1 2 3 4 5 6	X	F/34
	N	1 2 3 4 5 6	X	F/35
	H	1 2 3 4 5 6	X	F/36
	CE	1 2 3 4 5 6	X	F/37
7.4 Development and use of work-based assessment	F	1 2 3 4 5 6	X	F/38
	N	1 2 3 4 5 6	X	F/39
	H	1 2 3 4 5 6	X	F/40
	CE	1 2 3 4 5 6	X	F/41
7.5 Arrangements for monitoring assessment	F	1 2 3 4 5 6	X	F/42
	N	1 2 3 4 5 6	X	F/43
	H	1 2 3 4 5 6	X	F/44
	CE	1 2 3 4 5 6	X	F/45
7.6 Grade determination	F	1 2 3 4 5 6	X	F/46
	N	1 2 3 4 5 6	X	F/47
	H	1 2 3 4 5 6	X	F/48
	CE	1 2 3 4 5 6	X	F/49

Please tick this box if Section 7 **not** covered during visit ☐   F/50

8 Course review and evaluation

Key Issues	Level	Low Ratings (please circle) High	Not covered	
8.1 Procedures for course review and evaluation	F	1 2 3 4 5 6	X	G/26
	N	1 2 3 4 5 6	X	G/27
	H	1 2 3 4 5 6	X	G/28
	CE	1 2 3 4 5 6	X	G/29
8.2 Involvement of students and employers in review process	F	1 2 3 4 5 6	X	G/30
	N	1 2 3 4 5 6	X	G/31
	H	1 2 3 4 5 6	X	G/32
	CE	1 2 3 4 5 6	X	G/33
8.3 Formulation of an action plan	F	1 2 3 4 5 6	X	G/34
	N	1 2 3 4 5 6	X	G/35
	H	1 2 3 4 5 6	X	G/36
	CE	1 2 3 4 5 6	X	G/37

Please tick this box if Section 8 **not** covered during visit ☐   G/38

M063/4

Qualify in Management

Page 5
(rev 8/89)

Moderator no

Centre no

Visit date

For BTEC's use

Comments on issues not covered in sections 1 – 8

Space for continuation (if required)

Section no _____
continued

Section no _____
continued

Section no _____
continued

M063/5

Appendix C
Examiners' Reports

The following examiners' reports are quoted with the permission of the London Chamber of Commerce and Industry. They are selected from the 1985 Winter, Spring and Summer examinations and are representative of examiners' reports across the spectrum of professional examining bodies.

Advertising, Higher Stage

"It was clear that only those who had undertaken a thorough course of study and had read textbooks did well. Others, whose preparation had been poor, submitted meagre answers... a common weakness was when candidates did not answer the question and wandered off into irrelevant answers... there are still some candidates who insist on using colours when the question calls for a black and white advertisement [to be drawn]."

Arithmetic, Elementary Stage

"There was a disappointingly high number of failures, occasioned by failure to read the question carefully and [by] the commission of careless mistakes."

Business Arithmetic, Intermediate Stage

"The overall result was disappointing: while there were some good scripts, there were many failures, especially for overseas candidates.

This examination calls for the application of principles of arithmetic to business situations, but many candidates were unable to do this... they were obviously not ready for an examination at this level."

Business and Industrial Administration, Higher Stage

"A number of candidates completed only four questions this time. The very obvious result is that one fifth of the available marks are being passed over and this means that the candidate must score at least 50 out of 80 to pass; which often proves difficult."

"There was also a tendency by many candidates not to write enough — in a number of cases less than a page for each question... there is simply not enough that can be put in less than one page... Practical illustrations are useful, because they show that the candidate understands the implications of the question."

Business Statistics, Intermediate Stage

"Candidates did much better on calculation questions than on descriptive ones. Since most questions contain descriptive sections, candidates will not be able to score high marks if they ignore the descriptive parts of questions."

Commerce and Finance, Higher Stage

"A considerable number of candidates were not capable of producing five adequate essay aswers... largely due to insufficient knowledge... and a failure to appreciate the requirements of the questions... Candidates rarely attempted to explain their answers in terms of business reality."

Commercial Law, Higher Stage

"There was little evidence in these scripts of satisfactory application in regard to memorising the legal principles or applying them to fact situations. The candidates' approach to a complex subject was mediocre, at best. The presentation of work was not very satisfactory either: candidates are advised to complete their answers to questions on consecutive sheets and not to turn over a page in the middle of an answer!"

Company Law, Higher Stage

"Insufficient care is taken to give accurate answers."

Economics, Intermediate Stage

"The standard... varied from the excellent to the very unsatisfactory. Generally too many candidates ignored the mark allocation: for example in Q5, such candidates wrote a great deal on the main functions of money and very little on the determination of quantity (which attracted 12 of the 20 marks)."

Elements of Commerce, Elementary Stage

"Many failed to answer [the necessary] six questions. On the other hand, those who had adequate knowledge... often took the opportunity to display it and wrote far more... than was required. An example... was the request to name three types of retail shop: many described them in great detail and omitted the second (and far more mark rewarding) part of the question!"

Marketing, Higher Stage

"...far too many candidates gave the impression that their first acquaintance with marketing was when they read the examination paper! Others had memorised information which they tried to force into answers no matter how irrelevant it was.

"Many misread or misunderstood the questions and their answers had nothing to do with the questions. There were many wild guesses... Q3 produced... answers about the characteristics of packaging, or about packaging materials, without realising that the question was very specifically about designing packages to attract the customer."

Principles of Management, Higher Stage

"In general, candidates showed an improved ability to structure their answers to express their ideas clearly. Nevertheless, examination technique — the skill of answering questions — is something to which the candidates need to give continuing attention. There is a strong tendency... to answer... "Write all you know about...""

Public Relations, Higher Stage

"The main cause of failure was that candidates simply did not answer the questions either because they did not understand them or because inadequate study meant they were unprepared for such questions... There were a number who... dragged in irrelevant information just because it had been memorised. Knowledge must be displayed intelligently, not merely displayed.

"Failure to read the questions led either to wrong answers or the giving of unnecessary and time-wasting information. For instance Q1 said 'Write the opening paragraph'. It was surprising how many candidates wrote complete news releases decorated with headings, logos, dates and addresses (of which only the first paragraph could earn marks)."

Selling and Sales Management, Higher Stage

"Many candidates who failed this examination did not fail through lack of knowledge, but for the following reasons:

(a) failure to read the question properly and going off at a tangent on inappropriate arguments. Candidates should learn examination technique as well as subject content.

(b) Giving too short an answer.

(c) Not entering into any discussion upon examples and illustrations, ie candidates did not show evidence that they understood the examples they quoted. Many students would do well to adopt a "report format" in answering questions.

(d) Bad numbering of questions and candidates running one answer into the other. Candidates must leave a few lines after each answer and clearly number their questions; quite often there was a mix-up between question numbers and point numbers that they were referring to in their answers.

However, despite the above comments, many candidates returned reasonable scripts for this series."

Note that almost all of the comments are about examination technique, not about subject knowledge.

Appendix D
Examination Terminology

Be quite clear about the exact meaning of the following terms:

Briefly	Short, concise.
Compare	Look for similarities and difference — perhaps reach a conclusion about which is preferable.
Contrast	Set in opposition in order to bring out differences.
Compare and contrast	Do both of the above.
Criticise	Give your judgement about the merits of the subject. Back your views with evidence and/or reasoning.
Define	Write the precise meaning of a word or phrase. Quote a source if possible. Show that the distinctions contained or implied in the definition are necessary or desirable.
Describe	Give a detailed or graphic account of.
Discuss	Investigate or examine by argument, sift or debate, give reasons for and against. Examine implications.

Evaluate	Make an appraisal of the worth of something, in the light of its truth or usefulness.
Explain	Make plain, interpret* and account for. Give reasons for.
Illustrate	Give examples to make clear and explicit. Demonstrate understanding. Don't draw a picture!
*Interpret	Expound the meaning (or possible meaning) of; make clear and explicit.
List	Number of names, items, things; set out clearly in order.
Outline	Give main features, or general principles. Omit minor detail. Emphasise structure and arrangement.
Relate	Show how things are connected to each other and to what extent they are alike, or affect each other.
State	Present in clear, brief form (NB: brief).
Trace	Describe development or history of a topic from some point of origin.
Summarise	Give a concise account of chief points; omit details and examples.

NB: Note that standard English is used correctly in exam questions. Answer the questions asked.

Index

Action list	29
Assessment	
criteria	134
grading	127–9
reasons for	126
types	129–134
Certificate in Management Studies	
See CMS	
CMS	77, 84–8
Confidence	
gained from course work	22
Continuous assessment	
construction of course	96–7
failure unlikely	127
importance of integrity	95
people who influence success	101
value	51, 91, 95, 128, 193
Course	
consider as a game	16, 99
discipline	102
Course evaluation	
find out the rules	67
Course work	
always keep a copy	135
Data	
impact on mind	38–40

Determination	24
Double U principle	52
Employers	
report to them on progress	101
Examination paper	207–12
Examinations	
day of	199–206
decide to pass	191–93
disadvantages	93–4
do what you are asked	221
grading	91–92, 127–9
performance effected by pressure	116
preparation	193
revision	196
style	224
techniques	219
terminology	267–8
Examiners	
are human	105
characteristics	105
how to be noticed by them	109
Examiners' reports	219–221, 256–60
Fear	
advantages	17,
Flexibility	
of assessment	98
Fun	
getting it from study	23
Honesty	
with oneself	32
Incentives to learn	54
Interest	67
Interference	67
KISS principle	111
Knowledge	

use of	50–51
useless by itself	51
Learning	
attitude	49
best way for individual	23
demonstrated by behaviour	49
depends on effective memory	40
getting started	114
incentives	54
problems	118–9
skills	21, 51
techniques	22
theory	61
Management	
definition	75–6
judgement	93
Management courses	77–90
general principles	78–9
Memory	33–47
association of ideas	35
basic principles for improving	39
depends on learning style	40
hooks and triggers	237
how to maximise	35, 41
long term	34
personalise data	43
recall of important concepts	36, 42
recognition	37
review helps recall	59
short term	35
triggers and hooks	40–5
Mind	
functioning	37–8
impact of data	38
Mind-mapping	25–8
Motivation	
incentives	53

271

National Examinations Board for Supervisory Management
 See NEBSM
NEBSM 79–84
NEBSM Certificate 77, 81–83
Note making 70–71

Oral Interviews 236, 239–45
 objectives 240–1
 preparation 241–2

Panic
 avoidance 20
Passing examinations
 basic principles 15–23
 decide to 191–93
 pressures 16–17
 skill 16
Perception
 can be an asset 41
 role in learning 55
Personal development
 not noticed by yourself 137
Personal development journal 137
 content 140
 purpose 139
 value 139
Physical activity 59
Plateaux 66
Presentation
 content 230
 physical 234
 skills 222–7, 229
Pressure 16–17
 in exams 117
 handle using action list 29
 seek help from others 31
Pressure analysis 18
Projects 147–9

avoid tangents	156
choosing the tutor	150
don't under-estimate time	149
proposal	155
recommendations of	163–6
stages	154
strategy	151, 158–60
terms of reference	156
Question answering	217–26
Question spotting	213–8
Recognition	
leads to recall	37
Residential weekend	175–87
assessment	186
Review	67
as aid to memory recall	59
School habits	
avoid	102
Self-analysis	25–32
Senses	
use of	56
Skills	
learning	21
presentation	224–227
study	63–70
in subject	222–224
Strengths and weaknesses analysis	28
Study	
skills	65–71
Study plan	69
Subject	
knowledge	222, 232
Success	
in assessment	125
rules	135

Teaching
    joint effort 128
Textbooks 68, 79
Time
    management of 117
    required for projects 149
Tutors
    choosing for project work 150
    complaints about 119

SPECIAL OFFER – QUESTIONS AND ANSWERS BOOKLET

Determination and practice are necessary if you want to pass your examinations. Determination *you* must apply but we can help with practice.

As a purchaser of this book you are entitled to our booklet containing a representative selection of assignments from NEBSM and CMS with tutor's notes for the special price of only £1.95, including postage and packing.

Simply fill in the form below and post it to the address shown, together with your receipt or other proof of purchase and your cheque or postal order.

We can only accept applications on an original form and you must send the receipt.

Please fill in and return to:

> Paul Joyce
> Marketing Manager
> Bound Book Division
> Croner Publications Ltd
> Croner House
> London Road
> Kingston upon Thames
> Surrey KT2 6SR

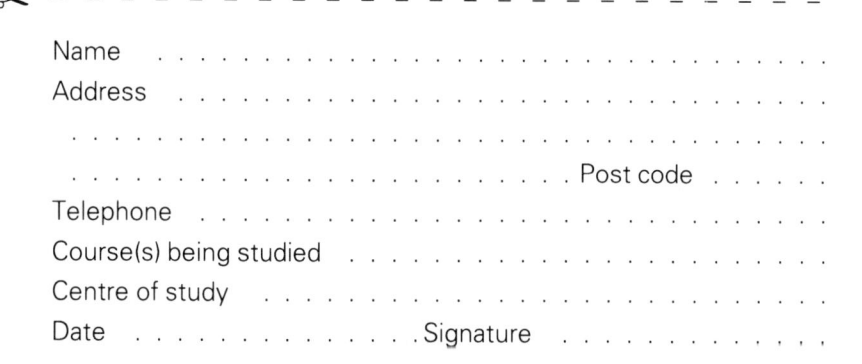

✂ —

Name . . . .
Address . . . .
. . . .
. . . . Post code . . . .
Telephone . . . .
Course(s) being studied . . . .
Centre of study . . . .
Date . . . . Signature . . . .